'This landmark book is an authoritative text on the organisation of support and methods of direct practice with people with severe intellectual disability. Written by two outstanding academic leaders, it draws together the significant body of research that forms the evidence base for person-centred active support. Its unique contribution and thus immense value is the clarity with which this knowledge is translated into a comprehensive guide to every day practice for staff, front line leaders and senior managers. This book is a key source of theory and evidence for students, researchers and policy makers, as well as providing practitioners and organisations with a blueprint for action.'

– Professor Christine Bigby, La Trobe University, Australia

'Mansell and Beadle-Brown have pulled together, in one place, a readable, practical yet research-based guide to improving support for people with significant intellectual disabilities. I recommend this concise volume for any service provider or policymaker who supports this population. It is well worth the read.'

– Steven M. Eidelman, H. Rodney Sharp Professor of Human Services Policy and Leadership, University of Delaware

'This is a really helpful book for anyone wishing not only to understand the place of person-centred active support in enabling people with complex support needs to exercise control over their own lives, but to implement it effectively. It is meticulously researched and distils experience gained from implementation really well.'

– Bob Tindall, former Chair and current board member of the Association of Supported Living (ASL)

'In my 35 years of working with people with a disability I have not come across anything as important as *Active Support.* It is now at the core of almost all the work that I do.'

– Gary Radler, Clinical Psychologist, Positive Behaviour Support Services, Australia

'*Active Support* has been an essential core element of what we do for more than ten years; it takes energy and tenacity to implement and maintain but the difference it makes in people's lives

– Ian McLean, CEO, Golden City Su

GW00771869

Active Support

of related interest

Group Homes for People with Intellectual Disabilities
Encouraging Inclusion and Participation
Tim Clement and Christine Bigby
Foreword by Professor Jim Mansell
ISBN 978 1 84310 645 6
eISBN 978 0 85700 205 1

Planning and Support for People with Intellectual Disabilities
Issues for Case Managers and Other Professionals
Edited by Christine Bigby, Chris Fyffe and Elizabeth Ozanne
ISBN 978 1 84310 354 7
eISBN 978 1 84642 617 9

Person Centred Planning and Care Management with People with
Learning Disabilities
Edited by Paul Cambridge and Steven Carnaby
ISBN 978 1 84310 131 4
eISBN 978 1 84642 140 2

Caring for the Physical and Mental Health of People with Learning
Disabilities
David Perry, Louise Hammond, Geoff Marston, Sherryl Gaskell and James Eva
Foreword by Dr Anthony Kearns
ISBN 978 1 84905 131 6
eISBN 978 0 85700 225 9

Active
Support

Enabling and Empowering People with Intellectual Disabilities

Jim Mansell and Julie Beadle-Brown

Jessica Kingsley *Publishers*
London and Philadelphia

Golden City Support Services and United Response have kindly granted permission for use of material in Chapter 6 and Chapter 7.

First published in 2012
by Jessica Kingsley Publishers
116 Pentonville Road
London N1 9JB, UK
and
400 Market Street, Suite 400
Philadelphia, PA 19106, USA

www.jkp.com

Library of Congress Cataloging in Publication Data
Mansell, Jim.
    Active support : enabling and empowering people with intellectual disabilities / Jim Mansell and Julie Beadle-Brown.
       p. cm.
    Includes bibliographical references and index.
    ISBN 978-1-84905-111-8 (alk. paper)
    1. People with mental disabilities--Services for. 2. Social work with people with mental disabilities. I. Beadle-Brown, Julie. II. Title.
    HV3004.M29 2012
    362.2--dc23
                                 2011049419

British Library Cataloguing in Publication Data
A CIP catalogue record for this book is available from the British Library

ISBN 978 1 84905 111 8
eISBN 978 0 85700 300 3

Printed and bound in Great Britain

Contents

Acknowledgements

We have learned from the experience of a great many people in the work reported in this book.

We would like to thank our academic colleagues in the Tizard Centre over many years, colleagues in the Welsh Centre for Learning Disabilities, particularly David Felce and Edwin Jones (now at Glamorgan University), Sandy Toogood (now at Bangor University), our research partners at La Trobe University, particularly Christine Bigby, Louise Mountford, Emma Bould, Sam Murray and Tim Clement, and other Australian colleagues, particularly Roger Stancliffe from the University of Sydney.

Collaborators in services providing support to people with intellectual disabilities have also strongly influenced our learning. Since the early 1980s we have collectively provided active support training in over 30 different organisations in the UK and in Australia. These have ranged from training of senior managers and staff in small organisations providing one or two services, through to training of staff in all services provided by a regional or national organisation. Overall, we estimate that we have trained over 2000 staff in the past 30 years. In many of these services we have not only trained staff but been involved in supporting the implementation throughout the wider organisation and training trainers so that the approach can be sustained over time. In addition, we have run introductory training for almost 100 people through workshops at the university, and all our undergraduate and postgraduate students are trained in active support and its implementation. Among these many collaborators we would particularly like to thank Bob Tindall, Bev Ashman, John Ockendon, Bob Isles and Su Sayer from United Response, Aislinn Hutchinson, Steve James and Jayne Kilgallen from the Avenues Trust, Ian McLean and the team at Golden City Support Services, and Chris Fyffe and Jeffrey McCubbery from Bendigo.

We would also like to thank the many people with severe or profound intellectual disabilities who have shown us that, given the right support, they can and want to live richer, fuller lives.

We would like to thank Agnes Turnpenny for help organising the manuscript for publication and Rachel Menzies from Jessica Kingsley Publishers for her patience and support. We would also like to thank Christine Bigby, who commented on the manuscript.

Finally, we would like to thank our families for their support in the writing of this book.

Preface

After many years of research and development, active support is moving into the mainstream of services for people with intellectual disabilities. People with intellectual disabilities, their families and advocates are beginning to expect support that enables individuals to participate as much as possible in the activities of their life, at home and in the community. Organisations that provide support are looking for ways of doing this well, with proven results. Funding agencies and regulators are looking for evidence that resources are being used to provide the best possible value for money and that the quality of life of people receiving support is as good as it possibly can be. Active support is an example of *evidence-based practice*, a long-standing goal in health and social care (Department of Health 1991; Sheldon and Chilvers 2000).

The purpose of this book is to draw together the available research about active support, along with the experience of academics and practitioners putting it into practice. Our aim is to provide a comprehensive account which can be used by families and professionals (including students) as a guide and a source to understand active support.

Many of the publications about active support that are already available are training materials. Although these offer a description of how to provide active support and why it should be provided, they supply only a limited account of implementation of active support in practice. There have been several recent reviews of research on active support (Hamelin and Sturmey 2011; Stancliffe, Jones and Mansell 2008; Totsika, Toogood and Hastings 2008), but published research suffers from several limitations. First, the formal requirements of research methodology mean that published papers are likely to describe situations where the researchers had a relatively high level of control over the way the service worked. In order to achieve this degree of control, only some kinds of organisations will have been selected. Second, the publication of research in journal papers is constrained by the rules of academic presentation, so that much of what the researchers learned is not set out. The published research itself is therefore a selected, filtered account of the work that has been done. Reviews of this research then typically apply a set of criteria to define which studies are good enough to be included and leave out those that do not meet this (often more or less arbitrary) list, providing a third level of filtering. For example, Hamelin and Sturmey (2011) identify 25 relevant papers but then exclude all but two of them from further consideration.

In writing this book, we wanted to draw on all the available knowledge and experience, whether from research or other sources and including the often valuable but unreported lessons from particular projects. Of course, this does mean that the book reflects our judgement about what those lessons are and our interpretation of the results, and there is a risk that we are mistaken. The rigour of research methodology reflects the recognition that it is easy to deceive ourselves about what is going on when introducing innovations in practice – about what has been done, what are the causal pathways and processes involved and what are the real results of particular courses of action. But, in practice, rigorous research cannot cover everything, especially in the complex world of social care, where many different factors work together to influence the outcome, which is itself multifaceted and complex.

So research is always used in the context of judgement (Rioux 1997). By presenting the available research and commenting on it on the basis of our experience, we hope to provide a coherent account that others can use as the basis on which to make their own judgements about how to use active support to improve the quality of life of people with severe or profound intellectual disabilities. In doing so, we expect others to build on, extend and improve the evidence base for active support.

CHAPTER 1

Introduction

The purpose of this book

'Active support' is widely recognised as good practice in services supporting people with severe and profound intellectual disabilities. Training materials have been available since the 1980s, many staff have been trained and it has been the subject of extensive research over nearly 25 years. This book is intended to bring together in one place a description of active support, drawing on both the authors' experience and the published research to explain why and how it has developed, what its critical components are, and how it can be successfully implemented.

This first chapter provides a definition of active support and explains what it is intended to achieve, before tracing its development from some of the early community care demonstration projects in England to its current formulation as 'person-centred active support'. The chapter also outlines the remainder of the book.

What is active support?

For people with severe and profound intellectual disabilities receiving services, it is axiomatic that, in many respects, their quality of life depends on the support provided by staff (Landesman-Dwyer, Sackett and Kleinman 1980; Rice and Rosen 1991). Through the provision of help and encouragement, staff mediate access to, and use of, the opportunities presented by the home and community. They control access to many materials and activities directly (for example, by opening or locking rooms) and indirectly (by setting out and preparing materials so that the people they serve can take part in activity). They make it more or less likely that clients will experience the reinforcement intrinsic to the task by the level of assistance they provide. Through the disposition of their social interaction, they reinforce either client engagement in meaningful activity or passivity and inactivity. They shape client behaviour by the feedback and reinforcement they provide.

Despite this pivotal role, staff supporting people with severe and profound intellectual disabilities are often largely left to their own devices. They do not receive much training or guidance on how they should support the people they serve. They are often providing support on their own or with co-workers who have had no more preparation or experience. It is perhaps not surprising therefore that the support staff provide is often very limited in amount and quality. Studies of care practices show that residents in staffed group homes receive facilitative assistance (that is, help to enable them to do something) for a very small proportion of the time – typically well under 10 per cent, or less than six minutes in every hour (Felce, Lowe and Jones 2002b; Felce and Perry 1995; Hatton *et al.* 1995c; Jones *et al.* 1999; Jones *et al.* 2001a). For people with the most severe disabilities – that is, people who need *more* help – assistance is received for less time – typically only about one minute each hour (Emerson *et al.* 1999).

The consequence of this for people with severe and profound intellectual disabilities is that they are unable to make as much use as they could of the opportunities presented in their home and the community. So a typical picture is that people spend the largest proportion of their day doing nothing – sitting, standing, pacing aimlessly about. Perry and Felce (2003), in a stratified random sample of statutory, voluntary and private community homes for people with learning disabilities in England and Wales, found that average engagement in non-social activities was 42 per cent, with a range of 1–100 per cent. People with severe and profound intellectual disabilities have been shown to be disengaged for a greater proportion of time: for example, Jones *et al.* (1999) found that people were disengaged for two-thirds of the time and Emerson *et al.* (2000b) found that they were disengaged for 80 per cent of the time (that is, for 48 minutes in every hour or for 12 hours out of a 15-hour day).

Active support is an attempt to change this, by providing enough help to enable people with intellectual disabilities to participate successfully in meaningful activities and relationships, so that people gain more control over their lives, gain more independence and become more included as a valued member of their community, irrespective of the degree of intellectual disability or presence of extra problems (Mansell *et al.* 2005). It is 'active' support to distinguish it from the kind of support people with intellectual disabilities often receive: either passive 'minding' or doing things for and to people, instead of enabling them to do as much as possible themselves.

Although active support was developed in staffed housing for people with severe and profound disabilities, its primary focus is on the relationship between the person providing support and the individual receiving it. This 'enabling' relationship is important in any situation and so active support is applicable wherever support is provided. This may include families supporting relatives in their own home and staff supporting people in residential settings, in supported living or outreach/independent living settings, in further education, in day care and in supported employment, as well as in the wider community in using shops and other facilities.

Although the nature of the help staff provided might be different for different people (so, for example, whether people can understand speech or not), the principles of the approach are likely to be of wider application than just for people with severe and profound intellectual disabilities.

Development of active support

Active support evolved from work carried out as part of the Wessex Experiment, led by Albert Kushlick, in the 1960s and 1970s. It was refined and developed through the work of the Tizard Centre and the Welsh Centre for Learning Disabilities and has been widely disseminated nationally and internationally. This section explains what issues have arisen in the development of active support and how these have been addressed by different groups at different times. It sets the scene for a more detailed description of what active support is and on what it is based.

A focus on engagement in meaningful activity and relationships

The starting point for developing active support was the extensive inactivity and isolation of people with intellectual disabilities living in long-stay hospitals in Britain in the 1960s and 1970s. Scandals and inquiries revealed many problems in these hospitals, including gross physical deprivation (overcrowding, poor food, clothing and environment), abuse (ill-treatment, theft of possessions, over-use of medication and restraint) and neglect and inactivity (lack of care, lack of contact and stimulation, extensive periods of disengagement and isolation) (Martin 1984; Morris 1969; Willer and Intagliata 1984). In a national survey of hospitals in England, Morris found that on the wards, the picture was of inactivity for all but a few:

> Without any shadow of doubt, and with the exception of the exclusively high grade wards and hostel patients, the great majority spent their day sitting, interspersed with eating. Only in very few wards…did we find nurses helping patients with individual or group leisure activities; nurses were usually cleaning either the wards or the patients, helping to prepare meals, cutting and washing hair, dressing or undressing patients or feeding them. When they were not so occupied nurses tended to sit or stand around talking to each other rather than to the patients. (1969, p.169)

The regime was essentially custodial, with staff using withdrawal of privileges or drugs to control 'bad' behaviour. This overall picture, of neglect, abuse and ill-treatment, of course persists in many countries now (e.g. Freyhoff et al. 2004; Mental Disability Advocacy Center and Association for Social Affirmation of People with Mental Disabilities 2003, 2011), including, to some extent, even those countries that have made most progress in reform (British Broadcasting Corporation 2011; Hakim 2011).

As the first community-based alternatives to institutional care began to be developed in Wessex at the beginning of the 1970s (Kushlick 1966, 1969, 1976), Kushlick and his colleagues began to search for a way of capturing the dramatic changes they were seeing in all aspects of the residents' lives. They were measuring skill development but were concerned to look at activity and interaction as well. They found this in the work of Risley at the University of Kansas. Risley was using direct observation to record the amount of time that children with special needs were engaged in appropriate activity in the classroom, and their interaction with each other and with staff (Hart and Risley 1976). Working within the newly emerging framework of applied behaviour analysis, this approach led to attempts to experiment with different arrangements, materials and staff behaviour to promote appropriate activity in services for young children and in nursing homes for older people.

Kushlick's team adopted this approach and developed observational measures of resident activity and staff–resident interaction suitable for use in institutions and community-based services for people with intellectual disabilities (Durward and Whatmore 1976; Felce, Kushlick and Mansell 1980; Felce, Mansell and Kushlick 1980). Their measure of activity focused on what they called *engagement*, meaning participation by the child or adult being observed in any meaningful activity. This included personal tasks such as eating or washing, social activities such as talking to or responding to other people and leisure and domestic activities such as playing games or washing dishes. The key point was that the person was doing these things, perhaps with help, rather than being the passive recipient of care. Staff interaction was measured in terms of whether it was positive (encouraging, prompting, helping), negative (reprimanding, discouraging, teasing) or neutral. Following Hart and Risley (1976), they argued that the programmatic elements of care actually took up a relatively small part of the day and that residents could spend large amounts of time waiting for their turn within activities and waiting between activities (Kushlick *et al.* 1976). They also argued that a major goal of services should be enhanced competence rather than just enhanced skills: that engaging constructively with other people and the materials and tasks of everyday life was more important than just amassing skills, which might in any case be lost if not used (Mansell *et al.* 1987b, pp.197–200).

Given evidence from American research that engagement in meaningful activity could be promoted by changing the way activities were organised and how staff provided support to people (McClannahan and Risley 1975; Quilitch 1974; Quilitch and Gray 1974), British researchers began to experiment with similar studies. Porterfield, Blunden and Blewitt (1980) and Porterfield and Blunden (1979) showed that if staff provided prompts and encouragement to use recreational materials, people with severe and profound intellectual disabilities attending special needs units in a day centre increased their level of engagement in meaningful activity. This was replicated in a special school class (McBrien and Weightman 1980), a long-stay hospital ward (Coles and Blunden 1979) and in a residential home for adults with severe and profound intellectual disabilities (Mansell et al. 1982a).

Despite the apparent ease with which it was possible to dramatically improve levels of engagement in meaningful activity by people with severe and profound intellectual disabilities, the studies by Coles and Blunden and Mansell et al. immediately raised questions about the way residential services for people with severe and profound intellectual disabilities were organised. What was the point of enabling people to engage in using leisure and recreational materials for short sessions each day, when this had no impact on the rest of their lives?

A new model of support

The implication of these criticisms was that activities needed to be the real activities of everyday life rather than specially set-up therapy sessions.

> Instead of doing all the housework as efficiently as possible, and then attempting to occupy clients for long periods of each day with toys, staff could perhaps be organized to spend most of the day doing housework with clients, arranging each activity to maximize the opportunities for clients with different levels of ability to participate. As well as substantially increasing the variety of activities available to staff, such an approach would also involve practising skills which (at least for most clients) were much more directly useful in their day-to-day lives. Such activities would be appropriate for adults and, even for the most handicapped people, may not have the negative connotations attached to child-like activities. (Mansell et al. 1982a, p.603)

Even for people with the more severe disabilities, ordinary adult activities could be made accessible by selecting the simpler parts of them (Felce et al. 1984).

The implication of this idea was that services needed to be redesigned to focus on enabling engagement in meaningful activity as a primary outcome, rather than being organised so that staff did all the activity and residents waited for access to leisure activities.

The goal of services should be to enable people to live their lives by providing whatever help was required. Bellamy and his colleagues, for example, offered a definition of *lifestyle* as a key outcome by which services should be judged, in which they included the extent of participation in activity at home and in the community, as well as other issues such as the individual's social network or the extent to which they controlled their lives (Bellamy *et al.* 1986, 1990).

The opportunity to apply these ideas in practice arose with the development of some of the first small staffed housing schemes for people with severe and profound intellectual disabilities in the UK, set up in Andover, Hampshire, in 1980 (Felce and Toogood 1988; Mansell *et al.* 1987b). These new services provided several important opportunities:

1. The people living in these houses were local people with severe or profound intellectual disabilities and a wide range of associated problems; people were not excluded because they were 'too disabled' to live in the community.

2. The houses were ordinary dwellings located among others in the community. They were furnished and equipped just like other people's homes (sometimes with special adaptations or better-quality materials to meet the needs of individuals living there) and were within easy walking distance of shops and amenities in the town. They did not use bulk purchase or official supply arrangements and the equipment they had was domestic in scale. Thus they provided residents with all the ordinary opportunities of everyday living.

3. Staff were employed knowing that they would work with researchers to develop better ways of supporting people with severe and profound intellectual disabilities to live their lives. They were newly recruited and most staff had no experience of more institutional settings for people with intellectual disabilities.

Working together, staff supporting residents in these houses and the researchers tried to construct a set of staff procedures that made most use of the opportunities presented by the socially and materially enriched environments. The metaphor was that the service could be thought of as a production system (see Figure 1.1). The product the service 'made' was the lifestyle experienced by the service user, and the task of the innovator was to construct a service that could deliver this outcome. The assumption was that poor-quality care environments, once replaced with adequately resourced housing in the community and all the opportunities that it provides, did not have mechanisms for working effectively with service users. The focus was therefore initially on inventing organisational arrangements and procedures that effectively enabled service users to make use of the opportunities provided by the location and setting of their home. The arrangements identified were for supporting engagement in meaningful activity and relationships, developing new skills, managing challenging behaviour and individual planning. As these arrangements were worked out, they had to be effectively coordinated, which meant not only making them consistent with one another (so that, for example, the priorities staff attended to in incidental teaching were those identified in the individual's plan) but also balancing the work involved in keeping all the elements working (e.g. not spending so much resource on person-centred planning that there is no time left for supporting people to do activities they want to do).

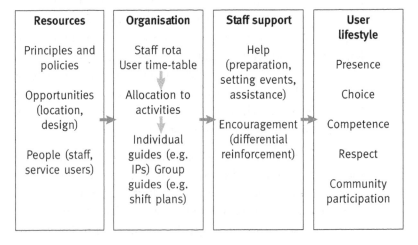

Resources	Organisation	Staff support	User lifestyle
Principles and policies	Staff rota User time-table	Help (preparation, setting events, assistance)	Presence
Opportunities (location, design)	Allocation to activities		Choice
		Encouragement (differential reinforcement)	Competence
People (staff, service users)	Individual guides (e.g. IPs) Group guides (e.g. shift plans)		Respect
			Community participation

Figure 1.1 The service as a production system (from Mansell, McGill and Emerson 1994)

These working methods were described in *Developing Staffed Housing for People with Mental Handicaps* (Mansell *et al.* 1987b). This was a comprehensive description of setting up and running a staffed house for people with severe and profound intellectual disabilities. It covered aspects of planning the home, such as identifying the people to be served, finding suitable property, adapting and furnishing the property, working out how many staff were needed, staff training, dealing with potential neighbours and managing the transition from wherever people were previously living. Like most of the very early staffed housing services developed for people with severe and profound disabilities, the model was of a property owned by a public agency – models of supported living were not yet developed. It also covered the way staff should support the people living in the house. This included individual programme planning as an overarching system of setting goals and coordinating activities, supported by specific procedures for helping people develop new skills, engage in meaningful activities in the home (such as preparing meals, doing housework, leisure activities) and in the local community (such as shopping, visiting family and friends and using leisure facilities) and for responding to and managing challenging behaviour.

Early results of this new model were quite dramatic. Mansell *et al.* (1984) showed that it was possible to support people to engage in everyday domestic activities in a staffed house organised to promote engagement. Six residents spent between 22 and 67 per cent of the available time in purposeful activity and between 27 and 65 per cent of this was engagement in housework or domestic tasks. Even the most disabled individuals spent more time engaged in housework than in leisure and recreational tasks. Levels of engagement in meaningful activity were higher than in institutional settings: Felce, de Kock and Repp (1986) showed that engagement in a three-hour period including the evening meal averaged 51 per cent for six residents in a staffed house compared with 23 per cent for a matched group of residents in institutions. When the matched group moved to a staffed house organised on the same principles, their engagement increased to 56 per cent.

Saxby *et al.* (1986) showed that when people went shopping or visited cafés or public houses, staff were able to support them to participate in the activity. Ten people in the two houses were accompanied on six shopping trips and three visits to cafés or public houses. On average, they were engaged in meaningful activity for 29 per cent of the time when shopping and 36 per cent of the time in cafés and public houses. Nine out of the ten people had contact with members of the public, though for small periods of time.

The marked improvements found by these quantitative studies reflected pervasive and substantial changes in many aspects of the quality of life of the people living in these houses. As Felce and Toogood explained in their book *Close to Home*:

> we also believe that much of the quality of the change in the lives of the adults…would go unrecorded if we had restricted ourselves just to reporting the information gathered by the objective research measures employed. Although our research data are important to us, it was the quality of the adults' experience which these data reflected that gladdened our hearts and encouraged us to believe that the service was developing in the right way. (1988, p.9)

Of course, these studies were comparing a completely new model of service provision with models that had gone before. It is not possible, strictly speaking, to attribute the changes to particular characteristics of the model – so to attribute the changes to staff providing a particular type of support to enable people to engage in meaningful activity – rather than to any other service characteristics. Later research provided the evidence that it was the quality of staff support that played a central role in improving engagement in meaningful activity.

Note that this does not mean that the model – ordinary housing – is unimportant. We do not believe that it is possible to provide a good quality of life for anyone in hospitals, villages, cluster-housing schemes or any of the other institutions that exist for people with intellectual disabilities (Mansell and Beadle-Brown 2010). By their congregate and often segregated nature, these settings limit the opportunities for people to achieve a good quality of life, in particular with regard to social inclusion, social relationships and self-determination. We do not support attempts to introduce active support in such places because we do not think that it can ever be person-centred. Ordinary housing among other people in the community is a necessary but not a sufficient precondition for enabling people to have a good quality of life.

Wider implementation

By the mid 1980s, deinstitutionalisation in the UK was beginning to take place on a wider scale. Influenced by the Ordinary Life movement (King's Fund Centre 1980), many public authorities were beginning to plan the replacement of institutional provision by staffed housing in the community (House of Commons Social Services Committee 1985). In the South East Thames region (covering South East London, Kent and Sussex), support for the development of community services (Mansell 1988a, 1988b, 1989; Mansell *et al.* 1987a) included new video-based training materials under the banner 'Bringing People Back Home'. These were largely based on Mansell *et al.* (1987b) and included modules on individual planning (Brown and Bailey 1987a), working with families (Brown and Bailey 1987b), developing new skills (Brown, Bell and Brown 1988), engagement in meaningful activity (Brown, Toogood and Brown 1987), responding to challenging behaviour (Brown and Brown 1988) and building social networks (Brown and Brown 1989). The module focusing on engagement (called 'Participation in Everyday Activities') was the first attempt to set out the staff procedures concerned with supporting engagement in meaningful activity separately from those directed at other areas of client experience. This module combined a focus on how staff should directly facilitate people's involvement in activity with tools for helping to organise the staff support so that such facilitation was possible.

In Wales, a national strategy for deinstitutionalisation and community living (Welsh Office 1983) led to the rapid development of supported housing in the community. Jones *et al.* (1996a) developed a series of training materials in active support based on the earlier work in Andover (Mansell *et al.* 1987b). In their materials, 'active support' was taken to refer to the whole group of interventions – supporting participation in activity, incidental teaching, structured teaching, individual planning and monitoring quality.

Both sets of materials were intended to be used to provide classroom-based training backed up by 'interactive' or 'whole-environment' training, in which hands-on training is provided to staff providing support to the people they serve in the places where they live (Jones *et al.*, 1999, 2001a, 2001b; Mansell, Hughes and McGill 1994; Whiffen 1984).

In a series of studies, Jones and colleagues from the Welsh Centre for Learning Disabilities demonstrated the effect of active support on engagement in meaningful activity by people with intellectual disabilities living in small group homes. In the first study (Jones *et al.* 1999), active support was introduced in five group homes. The amount of assistance people received from staff increased significantly with corresponding increases in engagement. Engagement and assistance were positively correlated and inversely related to adaptive behaviour – at baseline, staff gave more attention and assistance to the most able people, whereas after the introduction of active support, attention was unrelated to adaptive behaviour, but those with the lowest adaptive behaviour scores received more assistance. Gains in engagement were maintained in the majority of homes at six months and eight to twelve months after intervention.

A second study (Jones *et al.* 2001a) set out to replicate the 1999 study on a larger scale and introduced active support into 38 settings for 106 people with intellectual disabilities. On average, assistance received from staff almost doubled and this was accompanied by an 8 per cent increase in engagement, most of which was accounted for by an increase in domestic activities – there were no changes in social activity, contact from staff other than assistance or challenging behaviour.

Finally, Jones *et al.* (2001b) introduced active support into 74 houses in three voluntary sector organisations (188 people in total). In 22 houses, training was delivered by the researchers; in 16 houses, training was delivered by service managers with support from the researchers; and in 36 services, managers were responsible for delivering training themselves. The study found that in the majority of houses in the third group the training was not delivered as intended – in 29 of the 36 houses, interactive training was not carried out. Assistance from staff and engagement in meaningful activity by residents increased in the first two groups but not in the third, showing the importance of the hands-on training. This study also showed that active support was most effective with people with higher support needs – in particular with a score of less than 180 on the adaptive behaviour scale (Nihira, Leland and Lambert 1993).

This suite of studies showed that active support was effective outside the context of deinstitutionalisation, that staff assistance, rather than just other kinds of contact, was key to helping people to engage in activities around the home and community, that active support was most effective for those with higher support needs and that hands-on training was needed in addition to classroom-based training.

However, although these studies demonstrated the effect of active support on engagement in meaningful activity in services where there was a strong involvement by researchers, problems of implementation on a wider scale were also apparent. Mansell *et al.* (1994) describe an intervention to train staff supporting people with severe and profound intellectual disabilities in 20 houses. Classroom and whole-environment training was provided, administrative issues such as recruitment practices, induction training, job description and staff deployment were adjusted to promote the adoption of active support and managers were trained to collect data on engagement in meaningful activity using observational methods. Although trainers reported increased involvement in a wider range of activities and staff becoming more skilled at supporting people in the first group of houses, and the observational data collected by the service showed a rising trend, independent observational evidence showed no change over a 15-month period. Similar results were reported for seven houses provided by another agency (Mansell and Barrett 1993; Moore and Mansell 1998; Orlowska and Mansell 1996). In both projects, lack of commitment of managers, competing demands for priority from administrative activities and lack of skilled leadership for front-line staff were identified as factors contributing to weak performance.

In another study, Bradshaw *et al.* (2004) found increases in engagement in three houses, but these increases were due to the two most able residents in two houses and the residents in the third house. In three comparison houses, engagement levels actually declined. Lack of management commitment and lack of leadership were identified as problems. Mansell *et al.* (2002b) compared two matched groups of people living in staffed housing which were part of an organisation implementing active support on a wide scale. One group lived in homes where staff did implement active support, resulting in increased engagement in meaningful activity over a three-year period; the control group lived in homes where staff practice did not change and there was no improvement in engagement in meaningful activity.

Similar results were found in Australian services. Stancliffe *et al.* (2007) found significant increases in engagement, on average, in five houses for 22 people. Lack of change in one of the houses appeared to be because active support was not implemented satisfactorily, perhaps reflecting a problem with management. Fyffe, McCubbery and Reid (2008) looked at the implementation of active support in a similar group of services where active support training had been provided within the previous six months. They used accounts of staff, house supervisors and on-house-based managers in 11 services, each providing for five residents, but did not carry out observations. The main finding was that there was substantial variation across settings. The percentage of staff saying they had had active support training ranged from 25 per cent to 67 per cent (mean 46%). The percentage of staff indicating that changes in staff practices had occurred following the training ranged from 12 per cent to 78 per cent (mean 47%). The percentage of staff demonstrating a good understanding of engagement ranged from 36 per cent to 83 per cent in each house (mean 65%). Between 30 per cent and 78 per cent of staff reported problems with implementation of active support (54% on average). Although these findings are based on staff reports, this paper shows that implementation of active support is not necessarily straightforward and trouble-free.

Thus, the early promise shown by active support has been less evident in more widespread practice. Implementation has often been uneven or limited and this has been reflected in results which, though often showing an improvement over baseline, are not nearly as good as they could probably be, and may in any case be difficult to maintain.

Refocusing active support

The published research, and our own experience training staff and working with them on the introduction of active support, suggested that poor implementation and weak maintenance of active support reflected four problems:

- *Competing priorities.* Some staff did not see the value of engagement in meaningful activity for the people they supported; or, if they did, they saw other things as more important priorities.

- *Focusing on paperwork.* In some services, staff were mimicking the form of active support by filling in records and plans but not actually changing the amount and quality of the support they provided to the people they served. Active support seemed just to be about paperwork and no one was checking the quality of life of the people being supported.

- *Staff setting the agenda.* Staff were selecting the activities in which they wanted to involve people, directing the course of the activity and often providing support in a way that reflected their preferences and interests rather than those of the people they served.

- *Selecting only household tasks.* Although intended to encompass all the tasks of daily living, whether at home or in the community, staff were often only selecting household tasks. In particular, they were not taking opportunities to use active support to help people develop and keep relationships with people beyond their home and the staff who supported them.

These problems and what to do about them are discussed in more detail later in this book. They led us to revise our approach to training. *Person-Centred Active Support* (Mansell *et al.* 2005) tried to shift the emphasis away from staff and paperwork to focus on the experience of the person being supported. In particular, *Person-Centred Active Support* included more attention to:

- teaching people principles and rationales rather than procedures

- the importance of engagement in meaningful activity *and relationships* in the home *and* in the community

- the reasons why engagement is important and the common excuses made for not supporting people to participate in activity

- focusing on the way they support the person more than on planning and recording, in particular:

  ○ the use of all opportunities arising during the person's day (*Every moment has potential*) rather than just a few activities chosen by staff

- managing the level of demands on the person being supported by offering many opportunities to participate for relatively short periods (*Little and often*)

- replacing a strict hierarchy of levels of assistance with finding the kind of assistance the person likes best and rapidly moving to whatever level of help is needed (*Graded assistance to ensure success*)

- taking account of the preferences and agendas of the person being supported and emphasising the importance of *Maximising choice and control*

- emphasising the importance of coaching by the first-line manager as a *practice leader* in helping staff shape up the quality of the support they provide

- delivering the motivation to support good staff performance through managers taking an interest in client experience, not in record-keeping and paperwork

- aligning organisational priorities, policies and procedures to promote rather than undermine active support.

As in the earlier training materials produced by the Tizard Centre (Brown *et al.* 1987), the focus of *Person-Centred Active Support* remained on support to enable engagement in meaningful activity and relationships rather than (as in the materials developed by Jones *et al.* 1996a) individual planning, or structured or incidental teaching programmes. These (and other) aspects of providing support to people with intellectual disabilities can be done in different ways without changing the way active support is provided. They should be coordinated with active support but are logically and in practice independent of it.

Outline of the book

The rest of the book explores active support in more detail, describing it and bringing together research and experience to explain what works and why, and what might be the areas for future development.

Engagement in meaningful activity and relationships

Chapter 2 begins with the definition of engagement and considers the range and nature of activities with which people may need support across different settings. It explains the inclusion of a focus on relationships as well as on activities and considers the rationale for judging services by the quality of the lived experience of the people supported. This section of the chapter explains the nature of engagement as underpinning many aspects of quality of life as it has been conceptualised by the international panel of experts (Schalock *et al.* 2002) and as a method of operationalising policy principles. The second part of this chapter reviews the evidence that engagement is generally relatively low for people with intellectual disabilities in community-based and family settings, as it was in institutional settings, acknowledging that there is a strong relationship between the level of engagement and the severity of disability.

The enabling relationship

Chapter 3 focuses on various aspects of the relationship between carers and the people they are supporting. It highlights the importance of values and attitudes of carers towards people with disabilities, and in particular towards those with severe and profound disabilities, and explores the rapport and style needed for a successful enabling relationship. It then describes the four essential elements of active support (*Every moment has potential*; *Little and often*; *Graded assistance to ensure success*; and *Maximising choice and control*) and provides the evidence base for their importance and their effectiveness.

Organising staff support

Having introduced the nature of active support and what it looks like in terms of the day-to-day support of staff, Chapter 4 considers what is necessary in terms of organising carers to support one or more people with intellectual disabilities. It explores the need for routines, consistency and predictability and discusses the basic requirements for planning support and for allocating staff both in group settings and in more individualised situations. It explains different views and uses of paper-based recording and planning systems and highlights the key elements of monitoring practice and the use of observation in its widest sense to confirm that people's lives are improving. It considers the evidence for these approaches and draws on examples from organisations currently implementing active support.

Practice leadership

The focus of Chapter 5 is on what is needed on a day-to-day basis to support the implementation, improvement and maintenance of active support – a process that we have called 'practice leadership' by front-line managers and team leaders. The chapter starts by looking at problems of implementation of active support and what we know both from theory and from experience about the role of front-line managers in leading the practice of staff. It then describes what practice leadership looks like and the effect it has on the performance and experience of staff.

The organisational context

Whilst practice leadership by the front-line manager has been shown to be an important element in ensuring the success of active support, it is not the only important factor. Chapter 6 explores the successful implementation of active support at an organisational level and draws on both theory and the experience of organisations already engaged in the implementation of active support. It includes how organisations ensure staff have the skills needed and how they ensure that the motivational context is supportive of active support. Finally, it looks at the role of senior managers in providing training and support for staff and practice leaders, in ensuring that the messages staff receive are consistent and that they remain uncorrupted over time, in performance management and in recognising, rewarding and promoting good practice.

Integrating active support with other person-centred approaches

Chapter 7 explores the links between active support and other person-centred approaches such as person-centred planning, positive behaviour support, total communication, intensive interaction and the National Autistic Society's SPELL framework (see p.163) for ensuring an autism-friendly environment and approach. It draws from examples in organisations implementing active support to highlight successful strategies for implementing person-centred approaches in a coordinated and comprehensive way, at the same time making clear the central role of active support in successfully implementing each of the other approaches.

Conclusion

Finally, the book concludes by highlighting the main issues for those trying to put active support into practice, along with possible solutions for the difficulties that might be encountered. It also identifies the main challenges that have to be addressed in the research and development of active support in the future.

CHAPTER 2

Engagement in Meaningful Activity and Relationships

Introduction

What should services for people with intellectual disabilities achieve? This chapter addresses this question, using the framework developed by an international consensus panel as the basis for conceptualising outcomes. It then looks at how the idea of engagement in meaningful activity and relationships fits within this overarching framework. The idea of engagement is then explored in more detail, including some discussion of what makes activity 'meaningful'. Having explained why it is important and how it fits within the overall framework of outcomes, the chapter then includes a review of what we know about levels of engagement in meaningful activity and relationships by people with intellectual disabilities.

What should services for people with intellectual disabilities achieve?

In modern welfare states, the primary function of specialised services and support for people with intellectual disabilities is to help them overcome the effects of their disability, so that they experience the same quality of life as other people. Typically, this involves two kinds of intervention: attempts to help people overcome their impairments so that they can better manage the demands of everyday living, and adjustments to these demands so that they can live their life in spite of them. So services for people with intellectual disabilities attend both to helping people develop their skills and competencies to the greatest extent possible, and to providing whatever help is needed to enable people to live a good life in spite of their difficulties. The idea of organising services on a continuum following a *readiness* model – in which people could only live in more ordinary situations if they proved they had the skills to manage without help – has given way to a *support* model – in which everyone gets access to all the opportunities and benefits of an ordinary life with whatever help they need.

Since intellectual disability affects most areas of a person's life, the focus of help and support needs to cover many different issues or aspects of the individual's quality of life. These are summarised and presented in slightly different ways in different sources. For example, the English White Paper *Valuing People* (Department of Health 2001b) identified the four goals of services as *civil rights, inclusion, independence* and *choice*. The UN *Convention on the Rights of Persons with Disabilities* (United Nations 2006) establishes that everyone should enjoy the same rights, including the right to choice and autonomy, the right to live independently in the community and be included in their community, the right to access the same activities and facilities as everyone else, the right to participate in cultural, social, leisure and sport activities, the right to employment, to education and to health. Essentially, the Convention establishes that people with disabilities, including those with intellectual disabilities, have a right to the same level of quality of life as everyone else.

A consensus panel of the International Association for the Scientific Study of Intellectual Disabilities (IASSID) reviewed the different formulations of quality of life in order to develop an agreed set of dimensions which included all the different aspects identified in a single coherent, comprehensive framework. Figure 2.1 sets out the domains of this model and typical indicators.

Quality of life domain	Indicators
Social inclusion	Community integration/participation Social inclusion Residential environment Role (lifestyle and adaptive/problem behaviour) Supports (services and satisfaction with them) Acceptance Status
Physical well-being	Health (safety, healthy environment, physical condition, etc.) Leisure Physical well-being Activities of daily living Recreation Nutrition Mobility Health care
Interpersonal relations	Interactions (at work, with staff, etc.) Family Interpersonal relations Friendships (affiliation and loneliness) Supports (e.g. social networks) Intimacy Affection
Material well-being	Employment Financial Ownership Security Social economic status Shelter Transportation
Emotional well-being	Contentment (with work, residence, supports, satisfaction with community, satisfaction with services, etc.) Freedom from stress Emotional well-being (general, personal, psychological well-being) Self-concept Spirituality Happiness

Self-determination	Autonomy Choices Personal control Decisions Self-direction Self-determination Resident influence Self-advocacy
Personal development	Education and habilitation Skills Personal competence Fulfilment Purposeful activity Advancement/development
Rights	Privacy Respect Freedom Basic human rights Citizenship (voting, etc.) Access Civic responsibilities Activities related to local and national governments (e.g. partnership boards) Due process

Figure 2.1 Domains and indicators of the IASSID quality of life framework

In each of these domains, it is possible to use both objective and subjective indicators of quality of life. For example, it is possible to ask people whether they feel they have much choice and control over their own lives and also to find out how much choice and control they do really have. Although there has been a tendency to emphasise subjective appraisal of quality of life, both objective and subjective indicators are important. Subjective appraisal is influenced by people's knowledge and experience of possible alternatives (people may say they are happy or satisfied or in control because they are unaware of how their lives could be different) and there is also evidence that there is a homeostatic mechanism at work, whereby most people say they are broadly satisfied with their lives even given widely differing circumstances. It is also important to take account of the value that the individual places on particular aspects of quality of life, giving priority to the things that matter most to them.

The implication of the UN Convention is that there is no particular value placed on some characteristics, activities or lifestyles over others – everyone should be valued because of their *inherent* dignity – but that the same range of characteristics, activities and lifestyles should be available to disabled people as to anyone else. Within disability services, a different approach has been influential which does direct attention towards more specific action. This is the idea of normalisation, or its later development, social role valorisation (Flynn and Lemay 1999; Flynn and Nitsch 1980; Wolfensberger 1980, 1984). This holds that the main objective of services should be to create or support socially valued roles for people in their society (Wolfensberger 1984). This emphasis on social role reflects the adoption of a social deviancy model of disability. In this, the individual characteristic which is the primary difference between the individual and others (such as intellectual disability) is seen as overlaid by a secondary set of expectations for the behaviour and characteristics of the individual that reflect commonly held views about 'this sort of person'. Attention is therefore directed at the effect of these expectations on the person labelled as different, through the creation of circumstances that generally tend to confirm those expectations in a self-fulfilling prophecy. For example, if people believe that people with intellectual disabilities are childlike, they may speak to them in childish ways, dress them in childish clothes and involve them in childish activities. In doing so, they will increase the chances that other people will treat people with intellectual disabilities as childlike and that the people themselves will adopt childlike characteristics and behaviour, thereby confirming that people with intellectual disabilities are childlike.

Thus, the relationship between expectation and outcome can form a 'vicious circle' in which lower expectations result in lower achievement, which itself feeds lower expectations. For 'devalued' people, the expectations people have involve negative connotations and implications, which are conveyed through many different aspects of the organisation of services. The physical environment provided for people to live in (hospitals for the sick, zoos for the bestial, prisons for the menacing), the language used about them (subnormal, a headbanger, a vegetable), the kind of people around them (sick people and nurses in a hospital, religious devotees in a voluntary home), the activities in which the person is involved (playing with toys, watching children's television) and the symbolism or imagery used (childish materials and decorations, posters of animals, staff wearing keys on lanyards), all these act together to imply or require certain ways of behaving in the people concerned who, as they adapt to these expectations, justify them and encourage their extension.

The idea of normalisation is that this process can be reversed, by disrupting the expectations generated by the devaluing role. By creating and supporting a socially valued role for a disabled person, the goal is that services create expectations for achievement to which that individual and those around them will respond. The application of stereotypes by people around the disabled person is disrupted by their individual experience of that person.

Of course, it may be argued that it is not possible for people with substantial disabilities or differences to live up to the level of expectations which the wider society might value. However, normalisation, in Wolfensberger's formulation, was not about making people aspire to a valued role without help. Instead, it was about making the most of each person's potential and then constructing around them a web of support and help which enables them to fulfil the desired role. Some of this support would be in the form of services, but much of it would be informal and derived from the individual's access to mainstream opportunities and experiences in their community.

As well as specifying the goal as creating or supporting socially valued roles for people, the principle of normalisation has implications for the means or methods used to help people, since these too convey expectations and assumptions about the person. Given a choice, the principle suggests that the means used should as far as possible reflect valued roles. For example, it would be better to support someone interested in photography to join a club open to everyone rather than to set up a club at a day centre for people with intellectual disabilities. Thus, the definition of normalisation becomes 'as far as possible, the use of culturally valued means in order to enable, establish and/or maintain valued social roles for people' (Wolfensberger and Thomas 1983).

The extensive, elaborate and detailed guidance contained in Wolfensberger's evaluation instruments based on normalisation – *Program Analysis of Service Systems* (Wolfensberger and Glenn 1975) and *Program Analysis of Service Systems' Implementation of Normalization Goals* (Wolfensberger and Thomas 1983) was simplified by O'Brien (1987) as 'five essential accomplishments' (Figure 2.2) and this framework was widely used as the basis for staff training in intellectual disability services (Flynn and Lemay 1999).

1. Presence
The extent to which the service ensures that the person served is present in the mainstream of social arrangements for living, working and leisure.
2. Choice
The autonomy of the individual, both in making decisions about everyday issues and in determining the major directions of their life.
3. Competence
The personal growth of the individual in competence and experience, including the level and variety of activities in which the service helps the person participate.
4. Participation
The range and variety of friendships and other relationships the person possesses.
5. Respect
The experience of being valued by other people as an individual member of their group and the perception of the individual by other people.

Figure 2.2 O'Brien's five accomplishments of services

Normalisation has been misunderstood in various ways (Wolfensberger 1980). It has also been criticised for its emphasis on meeting the expectations of the dominant culture (Brown and Smith 1992) and therefore for its failure to respect diversity and individual human rights. It has also been suggested that aspiring to valued social roles may have negative psychological consequences for the individual (Emerson 1990; Szivos 1991; Szivos and Griffiths 1990; Szivos and Travers 1988). These concerns have meant that normalisation or social role valorisation have played a much less prominent role in intellectual disability services since the early 1990s. It does, however, offer a guide or a qualification to the rights-based approach of the UN

Convention – everyone ought to be respected as a person no matter how different they are, but it is probably better to emphasise their common humanity as much as any difference.

Lived experience is critical to quality of life

Within the overall framework presented by the concept of quality of life, it is possible to make a distinction between aspects that reflect status or circumstances and those that reflect the experience of day-to-day life. For example, *citizenship* might be indicated by someone's name being on the register of electors, or it might be indicated by someone going to vote. *Skills* might be indicated by the qualifications people have or how well they score on an assessment, or it might be indicated by people using the skills they have in their everyday life. We see the lived experience of everyday life as the more important of these: quality of life is, surely, about how people live.

Thus, for example, *personal development* is only likely to be possible if the individuals participate in activities that broaden their experience and allow them to develop new skills and interests; *interpersonal relations* and *social inclusion* depend on interacting with other people, as well as being supported to be present and participating within the community – engaging in activities with other people creates opportunities for interaction and conversation and for common interests to develop; *physical health* depends on lifestyle and activity; *material well-being* is improved if people are supported to find and keep a job or make use of the transport facilities to which they have access; *self-determination* can only be achieved if people have options to choose from, the experience with which to make the choices and an accessible method of communication with which to make their choices known – central to doing this is access to and support in trying new things and in finding ways to communicate choices; *emotional well-being* is sustained by participation in activities and relationships which leads to an increase in self-worth and self-esteem and in the respect with which individuals are viewed by others.

The extent to which people with intellectual disabilities take part in the activities of daily living, including the relationships that form part of their lives, is therefore a key measure of their quality of life. It is this that lies behind the idea of engagement in meaningful activity and relationships as the focus of active support.

Engagement in meaningful activity and relationships

Engagement in meaningful activity and relationships means taking part in any activity or interacting with other people in a way that is purposeful. Typically, it involves people (1) doing something constructive with materials (such as washing the dishes, cutting the grass, putting items in the trolley in the supermarket), (2) interacting with people (talking with people, listening to other people talking or attending to them while they show something) or (3) joining in group activities such as watching the ball and running after it in a game of football. It is a rather simple, even crude, idea that reflects the contrast with the barren emptiness of people's lives in institutions, where people were largely *disengaged*, meaning that they were literally doing nothing (sitting, standing, pacing about) or their activity was not purposeful (repetitive, aimless behaviour or challenging behaviour).

It is worth separating out the four terms in the phrase – *engagement, meaningful, activities* and *relationships* – and explaining in more detail what each means in the context of the overall approach.

Engagement

Engagement means taking part in the activity (in some writing, the phrase *participation in meaningful activity* is used to mean the same thing). The contrast here is twofold. First, taking part can be contrasted with doing nothing – with just sitting, or standing, or walking about of the kind commonly seen in long-term care settings for disabled and elderly people. Second, it can be contrasted with being the passive recipient of care activities. So, for example, the person sitting still while a member of staff combs his or her hair is not engaged in the task. The member of staff is engaged – but not the person whose hair is being combed.

Many people with severe and profound intellectual disabilities will not be able to carry out all of an activity. For example, they may be able to select items from the shelves in a supermarket but not be able to make payment. The point of active support is that staff can support people to take part to whatever extent they are able – what has been called *partial participation* (Brown *et al.* 1979). So it is not necessary to deny people access to an activity just because they cannot do all of it. They can take part in those parts of the activity that they can do, and someone with them can fill in the rest. This applies not just to sequences of steps (such as planning the shopping, getting to the shops, selecting the items, making payment, returning home, putting the shopping away) but also to individual elements of the activity. Even complex activities have some simpler elements which the person may be able to do. For example, he or she may be able to cut the lawn with an electric mower if someone else makes sure that the cable is kept clear (or if the mower is cordless).

Partial participation may be the result of limited skill but it may also reflect limited motivation. People may find it too difficult to take part in a whole activity. They may need to pace themselves, joining in at some times and not at others, or pausing at frequent intervals, or sometimes taking the initiative, sometimes following someone else's lead. Mansell *et al.* (2005) give the example of a man with profound intellectual disabilities being supported to peel potatoes. After he removes the first strip of peel, he appears agitated, gets up and walks out of the room. The member of staff supporting him might have thought that this meant he wasn't interested and she could have given up or finished the job herself. Instead, she sat peeling the potatoes slowly. After a few minutes, the man returned and carried on where he had left off. This pattern was repeated throughout the activity. By returning to the activity, the man showed he wanted to do it, even if he needed to take frequent breaks.

The point is that these limitations of skill or motivation are reasons for helping people participate at their own pace, in the parts of the activity they feel comfortable with, providing whatever help they need, rather than denying people the opportunity to be involved at all because they can't do everything on their own.

A special consideration arises when people are thought to be engaged in an activity even where there is nothing in their behaviour to confirm this – so, for example, when people are thinking about something or listening to music. People often want to say that the person is 'engaged' because they are doing, or might be doing, these things. Our view about this is entirely pragmatic. If people are not showing any behaviour that makes plain that they are doing something, then it is not possible to distinguish participation from, for example, sleeping. So we use 'engagement' only to refer to participation that is observable. If people do spend time thinking about something or listening to music, then, when considering the quality of their life throughout the whole day, this is unlikely to amount to much time. If, however, people are spending large amounts of time doing nothing, it is worth asking whether they really are thinking or listening to music and whether their life could be richer if they were supported to do other activities.

Meaningful

Meaningful, or purposeful, to whom? Some of the activities that people with severe and profound intellectual disabilities do – such as repetitive twiddling of a lace or playing with a rattle – might have meaning for them. People may gain comfort or stimulation from them, for example. This is not what 'meaningful' means in the phrase 'engagement in meaningful activity and relationships'. Here it means activity that is likely to increase the person's independence and control over his or her environment and to develop and sustain the relationships he or she has with other people.

In practical terms, people with severe and profound intellectual disabilities do not lead such busy and eventful lives that they cannot spend some time doing activities that they like but which do not seem to be meaningful. But if people spend most of their time in these activities, it ought to raise the question of how they can be involved in other things too.

Activity

Which activities? The idea of active support is that all activities should be available to people with intellectual disabilities, irrespective of the severity of their intellectual disability or the presence of other problems such as poor health or challenging behaviour.

One of the most common explanations offered by staff for extensive inactivity of people with severe and profound intellectual disabilities is that people are 'choosing' to do nothing. How to balance the right to choose with the right to participate is therefore a central issue for staff providing support to people with intellectual disabilities.

Choice does not trump all other outcomes: there are many situations where staff override the expressed preferences of the people they support because they judge that it is in the person's best interests to do so. For example, people with profound intellectual and multiple disabilities may turn their head away from a spoonful of food presented to them at a meal. Does this mean that they have had enough food, that they do not like the food, that they need time to swallow the previous mouthful? In every case like this, staff have to weigh up the different possibilities, try out different approaches and make a judgement about the importance of the result they achieve. They do this given their knowledge of the person they are supporting, the person's preferences and the extent to which the person is in possession of all the facts.

Spending long periods disengaged from activities and relationships is bad for physical and mental health and means that people are living impoverished lives, but it is not immediately life-threatening. There is therefore no case for forcing people to take part in activities they do not want to do. There is, though, a case for putting a lot of effort into coaxing people into taking part, for four reasons:

1. To the extent that people with intellectual disabilities have led lives characterised by limited experience, so that the opportunity to take part in most activities of everyday living has been denied them, they do not know whether they will enjoy taking part.

2. A history of failure, of not being able to succeed at activities attempted, or being discouraged, criticised or reprimanded, undermines self-confidence and motivation and may lead people to decline opportunities they would enjoy.

3. Limited expressive communication means that interpreting a decision not to take part is difficult. The person might be saying 'not now' or 'not this way' rather than 'not at all, ever'. Presenting opportunities in a different way or at a different time might get a different result.

4. If people are not used to being asked what they want, or do not have much experience of people paying attention to their preferences, they may not know what the consequences are of ignoring a request or an offer to take part in an activity.

Thus, choosing well is something that people learn. As Mansell *et al.* point out:

> 'Choice' is a loosely used term in this context: better to distinguish between different conditions of choosing. We

say that someone chooses to do one activity rather than another when they can do both (they have the skills, resources and time and they control access to each option)... For people who have difficulty expressing their preferences, whose range of experience is limited, and whose ability to control their environment is severely impaired, failure to create opportunities for participation is just as 'controlling' as setting up only one option. It ensures that people can only do nothing. The goal should therefore be to find ways of enabling people to express their preferences, to ensure that they routinely experience a wide range of different circumstances and to arrange their environment so they can control it. Only as these conditions are fulfilled can one say that people are in some sense making informed choices. (1987b, p.200)

What kind of activity? Active support was developed in small group homes for adults with severe and profound intellectual disabilities and almost all of the research on it has focused on activity within the home. This has led some people to think that active support is helping people to do housework. In fact, the methods involved should work in other kinds of setting (such as supported employment) and with any activities.

Sometimes, people with severe and profound intellectual disabilities are only offered opportunities to get involved in childish activities (such as playing with pre-school toys) or activities deemed to have some therapeutic value (such as being given different textures to feel). These kinds of activities are often chosen because people believe that only they are simple enough for very disabled people to do. This confuses simplicity with childishness. There are many activities or parts of activities in adult life that are simple, and many toys and recreational materials require a level of symbolic competence not possessed by people with severe and profound intellectual disabilities (Felce *et al*. 1984).

Restricting opportunities to recreational activities also constrains the variety of things in which people can get involved. If a person can already do the task involved in the activity, then it is often completed quickly and even a large stock of materials cannot prevent the same activities being presented to the individual again and again in the course of the day or week. An exclusive focus on recreation seems also to pose a number of problems of motivation. It is open to the influence of social pressures (either directly experienced by users or mediated by staff perceptions of the worth of the activity and the effort it merits) that it is trivial, time-filling and meaningless. Does it matter how fast people complete jigsaws or stack blocks? It may also be that recreational activities, since they are not linked into the sequence of essential daily activities, depend more for their motivation on staff to encourage participation at each stage than on any intrinsic sense of achievement or any obvious indication of what comes next.

Social role valorisation suggests that it would be better, given a choice, to focus on activities that show the person being supported in a good light – as a competent adult worthy of respect. Sometimes staff avoid supporting people to take part in everyday household activities – such as cleaning and laundry – because they think these are too mundane or fail to show the person in a sufficiently positive light. Often this means that staff do the activities while the people they are supposed to be supporting are left with nothing to do. Of course, if there is a choice between housework and something more interesting or more valued, then the housework might have to wait. However, given the choice between doing nothing and taking part in activities of daily living (with whatever support people need to succeed and enjoy the activity), we suspect that most people would choose the latter and that successful participation in these activities does more to show people as competent adults than doing nothing.

Relationships

People with severe and profound intellectual disabilities may be present in the community but they are often not really part of it. Most of their relationships are with the other people they live with and staff paid to support them. Building a wider range of relationships is seen as an important goal for at least three reasons:

1. Good relationships are themselves a source of emotional well-being; feeling loved and cared for by other people, feeling respected, feeling that one is making a contribution compared with others are all indicators of emotional well-being.

2. Good relationships underpin the personal knowledge necessary for good support of the individual; given the complexity of some individuals' impairments, the only way of understanding their implications for supporting the person is to know the person as an individual. When it is argued that people are not worth spending time or resources on, that individual knowledge can be the basis of defending people's rights. This is the basis for ideas such as citizen advocacy and the 'circle of support' in person-centred planning.

3. Good relationships protect people from neglect, exploitation and abuse. Whether in care settings (Cambridge 1999) or in the community (Cornwall County Council Adult Protection Committee 2007), neglect, exploitation and abuse depend on covert behaviour. Being known by other people who are likely to be confided in, to notice problems and to act on their concerns is one way in which people can be protected (O'Brien, O'Brien and Schwartz 1990).

Good relationships with other people, including neighbours, friends and acquaintances as well as family members, co-residents and staff, are therefore important. The extent to which people with severe and profound intellectual disabilities are supported to engage in social relationships is just as important as their engagement in any task. Tasks will often provide the framework for building relationships but people will often need help to interact well with other people. For example, people whose speech is indistinct or very limited or who only communicate non-verbally may need the person supporting them to act as a translator; people may need help to undertake the reciprocal tasks that form the basis for neighbourliness – taking in post, clearing snow off a neighbour's footpath, keeping the garden tidy; people may need support to maintain contact by telephone, greetings card or letter, and so on. In these situations the task is secondary: the purpose of the support provided is to enable the individual to sustain an existing relationship or to develop a new one.

Engagement in meaningful activity and relationships is therefore an important indicator of quality of life. If people have a good quality of life, it will be possible to see this in the richness and variety of activities and relationships in which they are involved.

Research on engagement in meaningful activity and relationships by people with intellectual disabilities

Engagement in meaningful activity and relationships is usually measured by direct observation – by being with the people whose lives are being studied and seeing what they do and with whom they interact. Given that interest in engagement grew out of concern about very low levels of activity and interaction in institutions, it is perhaps not surprising that a major focus of research has been how much people participate. Many research studies have focused upon how much time, on average, people spend engaged in meaningful activity and relationships, and engagement was a key indicator of the impact of deinstitutionalisation in many studies based in the UK. In general, early research found that levels of engagement were on average almost twice as high in community-based settings than in small or large institutions (Emerson and Hatton 1994).

Appendix 1 shows the percentage of time people were observed to be engaged in meaningful activity and relationships in all the available studies focusing on community-based accommodation. The levels shown are those before any intervention related to active support (or, where the study used one, for the comparison group).

Some of these studies involved collecting data from the whole waking day (Emerson *et al.* 2000b; Hatton *et al.* 1995b; Mansell 1994, 1995), where the purpose has been to compare the overall effect of one type of service against another. For example, Mansell (1994, 1995) observed people in three sessions on separate days to cover the period 0800–1900 hours. Other studies have used shorter periods such as that before and during the evening meal, selected because household activities are more likely to occur then (Jones *et al.* 1999, 2001a, 2001b; Mansell *et al.* 2008; Stancliffe *et al.* 2007). There is some evidence that the early-evening period used in these studies is an accurate estimate of the pattern of the whole day if a sufficiently frequent observation interval is used (Mansell and Beadle-Brown 2011), though this needs confirmation through further research.

Although there is substantial variation both between and within studies and datasets in Appendix 1, it is possible to draw some important general conclusions. First, engagement levels are, on average, low when compared with the general population. Studies in different countries, using time-budget methodology, show that adults in the general population typically spend over 90 per cent of their day engaged in meaningful activity and relationships (Szalai 1972). Studies of people with intellectual disabilities show much lower levels. Across the 24 datasets available in Appendix 1, the average level of engagement was 39 per cent (range 17–70%). That means that, on average, people with intellectual disabilities in these studies spent 23 minutes in every hour engaged in meaningful activity; for 37 minutes in each hour they were disengaged. Of course, this masks large variation between individuals, but if some people are engaged for most of the time, others are engaged to a much more limited extent.

The second notable observation from these data is that there is no overall improvement with the passage of time. Analysis of the data from those datasets presented in Appendix 1 for which both adaptive behaviour scale (ABS) scores and engagement data were available showed that there was no relationship between year of publication and levels of engagement. When the data were divided into roughly equal numbers of sets from before 2010 (n=12) and 2010 and later (n=13), there was no significant difference (p<0.05) for engagement or for adaptive behaviour. This finding is replicated taking an earlier division of before and after 2002 (that is, just after the introduction of the new policy *Valuing People* (Department of Health 2001b) in the UK). Although it may be the case that people with severe or profound intellectual disabilities are experiencing improvements in their quality of life in other areas, when it comes to direct observation of engagement in meaningful activity and relationships, the evidence is that there has been no improvement over time.

Lower levels of engagement among people with intellectual disabilities reflect both their personal characteristics and aspects of the environment in which they live and the support they receive. Generally, the more disabled the people with intellectual disabilities involved in the study, the lower their level of engagement (Felce and Perry 1995; Mansell 2006). Figure 2.3 shows the data from Appendix 1, where there is both an average ABS Part 1 score and a measure of the average percentage of time participants were engaged. Although the relationship is not perfect, it shows a strong correlation (*rho*=0.82, p<0.001, n=24) across the different datasets. This strong relationship between engagement and level of ability was also demonstrated within individual studies. For example, Jones *et al.* (1999) found a correlation between adaptive behaviour and total engagement of 0.88 at baseline and Jones *et al.* (2001b) found a correlation of 0.75 at baseline.

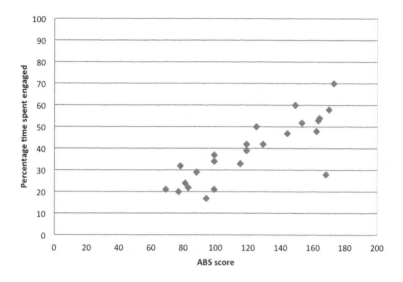

Figure 2.3 Scattergraph of engagement in meaningful activities and relationships by ABS Part 1 total score across 19 datasets for which data was available

However, in more recent studies, the correlation, although statistically significant, is weaker. Figure 2.4 shows the data at the level of individuals from the largest study yet undertaken (Netten *et al.* 2010). There is a significant correlation between adaptive behaviour and engagement (*rho*=0.493, p<0.001, n=360) but, as can be seen, the correlation is somewhat weaker. This is also true of other datasets – for example, Beadle-Brown *et al.* (2011) found a correlation coefficient of 0.566 (p<0.001, n=294). When the sample used is in general more able, then the correlation is much weaker – so, for example, analysis of the dataset in Mansell *et al.* (2011) revealed a much weaker correlation coefficient of 0.372 (p<0.001, n=109).

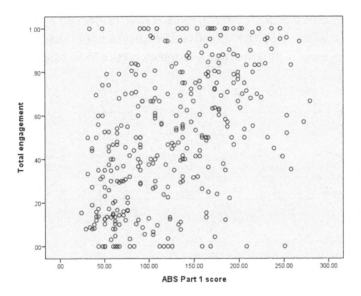

Figure 2.4 Scattergraph to show correlation between ABS Part 1 score and engagement in meaningful activity from the Netten *et al.* (2010) study

So although the level of support needed by people is a major determinant of their level of engagement, it is not the only factor that is important. In terms of other individual characteristics, the presence of challenging behaviour or autistic spectrum conditions does not seem to have much effect (Felce *et al.* 2011). We know that engagement also varies because of the kind of setting. Figure 2.5, reproduced from Mansell (2006), uses data from Emerson and Hatton's review of 46 British deinstitutionalisation studies involving 2350 people (Emerson and Hatton 1994) to illustrate that, on average, staffed housing achieves better results in terms of client engagement than small institutions, which in turn achieve better results than large institutions. However, the considerable overlap in the ranges of scores indicates that better large institutions can produce outcomes as good as weaker smaller settings, and that better small institutions can achieve outcomes as good as weaker staffed housing.

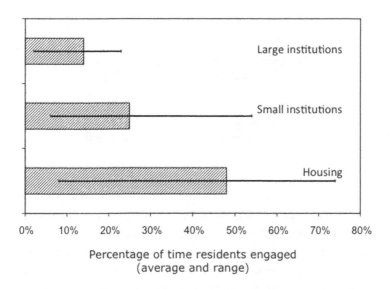

Percentage of time residents engaged
(average and range)

Figure 2.5 Variability in performance of residential settings in
England and Wales for resident engagement in meaningful activity
(from Mansell 2006, after Emerson and Hatton 1994)

The variation in results within housing-based services, once level of
ability is taken into account, also reflects the nature of the support
provided. This is the subject of the next chapter.

CHAPTER 3

The Enabling Relationship

In the previous chapter, it was argued that the extent to which people with severe and profound intellectual disabilities engage in meaningful activity and relationships is an important way of assessing their quality of life. Engagement levels were shown to be much lower for people with intellectual disabilities than for members of the general population, and lowest for people with the most severe disabilities. This chapter looks at how active support can help people to participate to a greater extent, focusing on the way in which the relationship between a member of staff or someone else providing support and the person being supported can enable greater engagement.

For people with severe and profound intellectual disabilities, help from other people is a critical factor in determining whether they can take part in activities and relationships. Without good help, people will not be able to access or organise things to do; they will not be able to undertake them and they will experience failure and dissatisfaction. The most important feature of active support is the nature of the help provided to the person with severe or profound intellectual disabilities. Other aspects such as plans, rotas and records only exist to deliver good support to the individual. It is the 'enabling relationship' that is the core of active support.

The first part of this chapter sets out what seems to be important in terms of the basis of the enabling relationship – the values and attitudes of those providing support, their 'rapport' with the individuals they are helping and their ability to reflect on their practice. It then describes the four essential elements of active support (*Every moment has potential; Little and often; Graded assistance to ensure success;* and *Maximising choice and control*), explaining their importance. Finally, the chapter summarises research on the effects of changing the way staff provide support on the level of engagement of people with severe and profound intellectual disabilities.

The basis of the enabling relationship

Whether staff (or other people providing help to people with severe and profound intellectual disabilities) adopt and use methods such as active support depends not just on their knowledge and skill but on their values and attitudes. If they do not see the point, or if they value something other than engagement in meaningful activity and relationships, then they are unlikely to adopt new methods of providing support. If they do adopt them, they are less likely to use them in the way intended.

There is evidence that, although staff agree with the values expressed in a policy of encouraging independence, inclusion and choice when thinking about people with intellectual disabilities in general, they are less likely to think these are achievable goals when thinking about individuals, especially more severely disabled individuals (Bigby *et al.* 2009). If people are not open to the idea that more disabled individuals can participate successfully, then it should not be surprising if they do not try very hard to enable such participation. Similarly, if people value the 'doing *for*' part of their role – caring for people, keeping them clean, well dressed, physically healthy – more than the 'doing *with*' part, then they may be less likely to create opportunities for people to participate and control the activities going on around them.

These are possible impacts of views about people with intellectual disabilities and the nature of the supporting task in general. The implication is that selection of staff with particular values and attitudes is important and that training and management ought to reinforce attitudes consistent with active support – something returned to in Chapter 6.

As well as selecting staff with values and attitudes that favour good outcomes for the people they support, families and managers sometimes identify 'matching' staff to the individual they support as important:

> Staff are recruited for qualities, not qualifications, to match
> the needs, personality and interests of the person they

support and the life they want to lead. There is, of course, emphasis placed on ensuring these staff get the appropriate qualifications and meet the National Standards. Partners for Inclusion believes that the first step is to get the right people and then, if necessary, support them to achieve required qualifications. (Fitzpatrick 2010, p.29)

Often – not always but sometimes – the best people have been people who have come with the right values and attitudes and with no experience whatsoever... That's why it is so important that the person understands and has that ability to build a relationship, to see the person as a person. You can teach all the rest. (Mother, quoted in Department of Health 2010, p.12)

Here the 'matching' relates both to practical interests – making sure that if the person with intellectual disabilities likes going swimming, staff employed to support them like swimming too – but also to an emotional sympathy. This is sometimes called 'rapport' and, in intellectual disability research, has primarily been a focus of interest in supporting people whose behaviour is challenging. Carr defined rapport as a relationship

...characterized by closeness, empathy, and mutual liking. In the absence of rapport, people may show little interest in interacting spontaneously and enthusiastically with each other...rapport-building is a critical feature of our approach to intervention. It is an ongoing part of the intervention, not just a stage that occurs once at the beginning and is then dropped. Furthermore, rapport-building is not a mechanical set of procedures but is based on sharing, cooperation and mutual give-and-take. (1994, p.111)

McLaughlin and Carr (2005) studied rapport with three people with intellectual disabilities and eight staff in one group home. Rapport was measured using preferences expressed by the people with intellectual disabilities as to which staff they wanted to support them, staff ratings of their own relationship with the disabled person (whether it was satisfying, enjoyable, interesting, warm, balanced and open) and ratings by staff of other staff. They found that when rapport was good, levels of challenging behaviour were lower, and that when staff were helped to improve rapport, there was a reduction in challenging behaviour and an increase in participation in the presence of staff who had previously been identified as having poor rapport with participants. The implication is that, as well as having personal values and attitudes that support engagement, good rapport will increase the likelihood that people are able to participate in activities and less likely that they present challenging behaviour.

Guthrie and Beadle-Brown (2006) report findings from a qualitative study exploring perceptions of good and poor rapport amongst professionals, staff and service users in intellectual disability services. One indicator of poor rapport in services, consistent across the focus groups, was when a support worker takes over and acts without consulting the individual he or she supports. The result of this type of behaviour was generally seen to be some form of challenging behaviour. Although service users found it very difficult to give examples of what happened when rapport was good, professionals and staff were able to do so. One of the key indicators was that staff would empower people, listen to them and involve them in tasks, as well as talk to them and share things about themselves. Figure 3.1 below summarises the indicators of poor and good rapport as perceived by staff and professionals.

From the point of view of the service users consulted, one of the most important dimensions appeared to be whether staff supported the person and did things with the person, encouraged and enabled choice and motivated the person (good rapport), compared with whether they exercised control and dominance, ordered the person about, ignored personal choice and/or lacked flexibility (Guthrie and Beadle-Brown 2006).

A third characteristic of good support which appears to be important is that people providing support are able to reflect on what they are doing and consider how their own behaviour, feelings and thoughts are influencing, and being influenced by, the person they are supporting and what is happening. That is, they need to be able to reflect critically on the relationship they have with the person they are supporting as they are doing so. One approach to this has been to teach staff techniques of 'mindfulness'. For example, Singh *et al.* (2004) showed that when three staff were trained in mindfulness techniques, the three people with profound intellectual and multiple disabilities they supported showed greater happiness than when with three other staff. In another study, learning increased and challenging behaviour reduced after staff were trained in these techniques (Singh *et al.* 2006). Mindfulness has also been identified as a possible intervention for reducing stress in staff working with people whose behaviour is challenging (see, for example, Noone and Hastings 2010). Singh *et al.* (2011) conceptualise mindfulness both as an outcome (awareness) and as a process (practice). The element most relevant in this context is *mindful practice*, which Shapiro and Carlson (cited in Singh *et al.* 2011, p.4) describe as 'the system of practice of intentionally attending in an open, caring and discerning way, which involves both knowing and shaping the mind'.

Poor rapport
- Carer uses negative forms of body language such as facial expressions and rolling eyes
- Carer talks about service users in front of them, talks over them and speaks for them, and does not allow service users to respond
- Racism, prejudice and dishonesty by both parties
- Carer adopts parent–child (carer–service user) style of interaction: 'Are we ready to eat our dinner?', when carer not going to eat
- Service user is non-compliant and engages in self-stimulatory behaviour

High rapport
- Carer asks service users for help, is empowering and allows them to say when they do not like/want something
- Carer demonstrates openness and trust, shares things about self and has holistic view of the person's needs
- Service user talks and asks about the carer in his or her absence, smiles when his or her name is mentioned
- Service user buys gifts or gives presents to carer
- Service user is able to ask carer for help and ask his or her questions

---

Figure 3.1 Summary of indicators for poor and high rapport from staff and professionals (reproduced from Guthrie and Beadle-Brown (2006), p.28)

These areas of research and experience suggest that the *technical* aspects of good support – the ways of helping the person with intellectual disabilities to engage more fully in life – may depend in part on the *interpersonal* aspects of the relationship between the person supporting and the person being supported (Donabedian 1980, p.4). In the absence of good interpersonal relations, it is less likely that the technical aspects of support will be delivered effectively. The enabling relationship is founded in understanding, respect and empathy for the individual being supported, a commitment to and understanding of the possibilities for a better life, and a reflective, critical appraisal of how things are going. This is a more demanding and more creative role than the task-orientated control, or even the pretend friendship that often characterises the direct support role (O'Brien, undated).

Essentials of active support

For most people with severe and profound intellectual disabilities, the reality of their disability is that, even if there are opportunities for them to initiate and take part in activities and relationships, they will not be able to do so without help from others. What should staff do to enable people to choose and take part successfully? Mansell *et al.* (2005) frame guidance to staff as four rules or principles to keep in mind, to be used with creativity and common sense. These are not procedures to be slavishly followed irrespective of the circumstances but reminders of what is likely to enable people to participate successfully.

Every moment has potential

The first principle is that every moment has potential for participation by the person with intellectual disabilities. Instead of constructing special 'activity periods' when people are supported to join in and then outside of which people are left to their own devices, staff need to examine the opportunities available throughout the day and find ways of enabling the person to take part to the extent that he or she can. This is consistent with a strategy of *generalisation* (Horner, Dunlap and Koegel 1988; Stokes and Baer 1977), in which people with severe and profound intellectual disabilities and the people who support them learn to make use of many opportunities for engagement, rather than becoming dependent on narrowly conceived special events.

The agenda is likely to be set by everyday relationships and activities – encounters with neighbours, shopkeepers, tradespeople and members of the public; housekeeping tasks such as shopping, preparing food, cooking, tidying, cleaning, laundry, decorating and gardening; leisure activities such as pursuing hobbies, attending clubs or using facilities such as swimming pools and cinemas; and the tasks involved in employment, education or other day-time activity (Mansell *et al.* 1987c; Saunders and Saunders 1998). Some of these activities are likely to occur every day, some less frequently. In addition to the tasks of everyday living, there are friendships and family relationships to be maintained through using communications media (letters, telephone calls, greetings cards, postcards, social networking using the internet, etc.) as well as visiting and meeting people face to face.

Within each of these activities, the person providing support needs to identify those parts of the activity that the disabled person can do on his or her own, those where he or she can do the task with some kind of support, and those where the task is too difficult or where the person does not want to do it. Where several people are together, then different people may be able to take on tasks of different complexity or difficulty. This process is analogous to *task analysis* (Kazdin 1989, p.310 *et seq.*), except that here the analysis is done not to identify goals for teaching but to identify support needs for effective participation. As noted in the previous chapter, the complexity of individual tasks is not the same as childishness and it is possible to identify adult contexts and activities of all levels of developmental complexity (Felce *et al.* 1984; Wilcox and Bellamy 1987a).

The support role then becomes one of enabling the person to take part in the activity successfully, varying the level of help to match that needed. Since many people will only participate to a limited extent or for short periods, support is sometimes there to bridge the gap to keep activities going. Mansell *et al.* (1987b, p.202) give the example of changing the blade of a food processor between preparing different foods – a relatively difficult task that is quick to do, where, if staff do it, the people doing the food preparation can get on with minimal fuss and interruption. Similarly, where the person with intellectual disabilities has problems of motivation or a short span of attention, it may be best to prepare the least interesting or most protracted parts of the activity so that he or she can 'cut to the chase'.

Analysing the flow of activity to spot opportunities for the person being supported to take part is something that can be done for an individual as part of a 'support plan' or a 'support profile' – a document or a video that records how the person likes to undertake a particular activity and the way he or she needs and likes to be supported. Useful though these may be, they are not likely to be a substitute for the skill of the member of staff in analysing situations moment by moment.

Little and often

New experiences are easiest in small doses. For people who may have a history of failure when they have tried to get involved in activities, or of being prevented from doing so (because there was nothing for them to do or because they were told not to), being offered the opportunity to get involved may not seem attractive. They may not understand what is being suggested, they may be anxious and they may ignore or refuse initial attempts to involve them. If they do take part, they may have little tolerance for clumsy support, or they may not have the mental or physical stamina to take part for long.

The aim, therefore, is to coax people into participating so that they experience success and are more likely to take part (in that particular activity and also in other opportunities). The 'little and often' principle is intended to provide graded exposure (Marvin 1998) to reduce the difficulty or aversiveness of taking part and provide enough opportunities for people to learn that they can succeed.

In practical terms, this means that those providing support should take several steps to present the opportunity in a way that makes participation most inviting:

- They should respect the preferences and agenda of the person (so not trying to involve individuals in an activity they do not like, or at a time when they want to be doing something else). Preferred activities are associated with greater participation and less challenging behaviour (Clarke *et al.* 1995; Foster-Johnson, Ferro and Dunlap 1994).

- They should get the person's attention and use understandable language and communications as appropriate – signs, symbols, photographs or objects of reference, making sure that their non-verbal behaviour is consistent with what they are trying to say.

- They should avoid overwhelming the person with instructions, information or conversation, trying to make it as easy as possible for the person they are supporting to understand what is being suggested (Bradshaw 2001).

- They should have everything ready so that the situation speaks for itself and the people they are supporting have the best chance of understanding what is being suggested and how to make a start – that is, so that they can make a successful discrimination of what they need to do (Gold 1980a, 1980b).

If the person with intellectual disabilities appears to be refusing to get involved, staff should ask themselves whether the person has understood what was being asked of or offered to him or her. It might be that the person has understood and is declining the opportunity, but it might also be that he or she has not understood, or the time is not right, or that getting started is too difficult.

When people do start to join in, they may not last the course. Since the goal is that people enjoy participating, it is important to support participation even if it is only partial or lasts a short period. The expectation is that if people enjoy brief or very limited participation, they will, over time, participate for longer and be able to do more.

Given the likelihood that people will take time to find out that they can get involved in activities and succeed, it is important to repeat invitations. Many people with severe and profound intellectual disabilities do not get the chance to take part in interesting activities because someone says that when they were asked (often it seems asked once, a long time ago), they did not seem keen. If people are going to discover that they can succeed, they need plenty of opportunities to do so.

Graded assistance to ensure success

In order to increase their participation, people have to find it rewarding or reinforcing. Active support emphasises enabling people to engage successfully in meaningful activities and relationships through providing the right amount and type of support. That is, it uses *antecedents* to increase the likelihood of success, in an approach similar to an errorless learning strategy (Lambert 1975; Touchette 1968). The advantage of this approach is that it eliminates or reduces the person's experience of the aversive consequences of failure. It does the same for the member of staff supporting that person and it shows the individual as competent and worthy of respect to any other people present.

Although social reinforcement (encouragement and praise) can also be used, the primary emphasis in active support is on the intrinsic reinforcement of undertaking the activity or completing the task. Relying on social reinforcement risks encouraging *prompt dependency* (Hume, Loftin and Lantz 2009), where the discriminative stimulus for the next step in a sequence becomes the staff interaction rather than the completion of the previous step. Of course, in so far as the person providing support does provide attention, encouragement and praise, this needs to be contingent on engagement in meaningful activity and relationships so that its effect as a reinforcer is to strengthen rather than weaken engagement. Early research studies on engagement demonstrated that social reinforcement, coupled with prompts, was effective at increasing engagement for many people with severe and profound intellectual disabilities (Mansell *et al.* 1982a; Porterfield *et al.* 1980; Quilitch and Gray 1974).

The support provided needs to enable the person to succeed at what he or she is doing. It therefore needs to be graded so that it is at the right level and of the right kind. If too little help is given, the person will fail; too much help and the member of staff will be doing the task. As the activity unfolds, the amount of help needs to be adjusted to fit the particular task or step. Where a relationship with someone else is involved (for example, where the individual is being supported to make a purchase in a local shop), success is also important for the other party. The member of staff in this situation is also trying to enable the individual to experience a successful encounter that makes further social contact more likely.

The first 'level' of help of which staff should be aware is simple presentation of materials – making the situation speak for itself. Having said what the task is, or what to do next, by way of general explanation and courtesy and having got the materials prepared, staff should hold back for a moment to see whether the demands of the situation itself are enough to elicit the involvement of the person concerned. If they are not, then it is appropriate for staff to work up the hierarchy of levels of assistance until they find the lowest level that guarantees successful execution of the task. In early materials describing this approach, the hierarchy of assistance was summarised in phrases such as 'ask–instruct–show–guide' (Brown *et al.* 1987; Jones *et al.* 1996b; Mansell *et al.* 1987c) (see Figure 3.2).

Ask
If the person does not seem to know what to do, staff should ask them to do the task or tell them where to start. This level of help will be useful where the person concerned knows what to do but not quite when to do it; an alternative to spoken help may be simply to point at the task or at where the person should begin.
Instruct
If the person still seems unsure of what to do, staff can instruct the person what to do, either by way of explanation (if the person understands spoken explanations) or by extra cues and prompts (such as pointing to each step in turn as the person completes the previous one or taking away some of the clutter of materials in front of them). Since the aim is to provide extra help to enable the person to do the task successfully, brief and clear instructions or prompts are likely to be more useful than if they are buried in streams of conversation.
Show
Where this level of help is insufficient, staff can show the person what to do, either by demonstrating the task first or by doing it alongside the individual so they can imitate each step. Many activities lend themselves to this kind of side-by-side approach in which staff model the task.
Guide
Finally, staff can guide the individual through the difficult step or the whole activity. The form of guidance itself can vary from minimal help with positioning through to complete guidance in which the individual has no possibility of error.

Figure 3.2 The 'Ask–Instruct–Show–Guide' hierarchy
of assistance (from Mansell et al. 1987)

Although this is easy to remember and useful in staff training, it is an over-simplification and a clumsy representation of the skill staff need to develop. People will have individual preferences for the type of support they receive. For example, people might find instructions aversive (perhaps because they are distracting or because they make people feel criticised); in these situations it might be more helpful simply to point at what needs doing or handing them the materials for the next part of the task. For other people, problems are likely to arise with the use of physical guidance. People with autism, in particular, may not like physical contact and therefore staff may have to find another way to provide support that does not involve touching them or holding them: examples might include repositioning the materials and holding them for the person, rather than trying to guide the person physically through the step.

The point of these examples is that staff need to think creatively about how to provide the right amount of help, of the right kind, for the particular person in relation to the task or activity he or she is involved in. They should not slavishly work through a set of arbitrary forms of help. Nor should they toil laboriously through every level of help before getting to the one that is effective: as staff get to know the people they support, they will be able to identify the critical range of help for different tasks for each person. It is important to start with a little less help than the person currently needs so that he or she is always given the opportunity to extend his or her independence. In this way, staff are always creating opportunities for learning and, over time, they can reduce the level of assistance in response to increasing independence and greater ability to take control by the person concerned, in the process called *fading* (Kazdin 1989, p.43).

As they become more practised, staff should be able to provide varying levels of help as part of the flow of their interaction with the people they are supporting so that the shift between levels is imperceptible. Although this will look 'natural' to others, staff will in fact be constantly reflecting on the amount of help they are providing as against what the person needs to do the task.

Maximising choice and control

There is a growing body of research that suggests that, in addition to responding to individual preferences for activities, increasing choice may also lead to increased engagement and reduced challenging behaviour (Cannella, O'Reilly and Lancioni 2005; Kern *et al.* 1998). Increasing the extent to which people are being supported to exercise control over what they do and how they do it is not only a method of increasing engagement in meaningful activity and relationships, but also an important dimension of quality of life in its own right.

There is likely to be a basic framework of appointments and expectations that structures a person's life. This will include regular commitments (such as going to work, visiting family, going shopping) as well as ad-hoc events (such as appointments for tradepeople to call, one-off visits or favourite television programmes to watch). These commitments will vary in the extent to which they are fixed or changeable, planned or spontaneous. For people who need a high degree of predictability in their lives – for example, because of autistic spectrum conditions – it is important that the person providing support is aware of these commitments and organised to help the disabled person meet them. This may have implications for the organisation of support and this is dealt with in the next chapter.

Within this framework there will be many opportunities to choose different activities or to get involved in activities in different sequences. Decision guides, such as photographs of different activities in a folder, on a choice board or on a mobile phone, can be used to help people choose between different options. Although there is little research on the effectiveness or impact of using such decision guides in their own right, they are often recommended in guides for teaching and supporting children and adults on the autism spectrum such as the TEACCH (Treatment and Education of Autistic and related Communication handicapped Children) system (Mesibov, Shea and Schopler 2004; Schopler et al. 1981). They are also an important element of methods of augmentative and alternative communication for use with all people with impairments in communication. If staff frequently respond to preferences expressed by the person they are supporting, then the person will learn that there is a point to making choices and will make more of them. Similarly, within the activity, ceding control over the sequence of steps, pace or duration of the activity is often possible. If there are choices to be made (e.g. which sequence to select items from supermarket shelves) that have no important bearing on the outcome (the sequence does not affect the success of the shopping trip), then staff can follow the individual's lead; if the person seems unsure what to do next, staff could prompt for a decision (e.g. 'It's up to you' or 'Either would be fine') rather than themselves selecting what happens next. If the person ends the activity early, staff can go along with that and look to complete at another time.

As in the other areas discussed above, maximising choice and control is a skill on the part of those providing support. They have to judge when no choice is possible (for example, to keep the person they are supporting safe), when stopping the activity means that the person has had enough or whether it means that he or she wants a break and then to return, when offering a choice would interrupt the flow of the activity or distract from the main purpose, and so on. This requires an awareness both of the person they are supporting and of the risks involved in particular activities. Managing risk so that people can still live their lives to the full is often a challenge for service-providing organisations and families but it is an essential part of providing support.

A virtuous circle enabling engagement

Providing active support using these four principles creates a virtuous circle in which each element strengthens the success of the next (see Figure 3.3). It reduces the difficulty of getting engaged in meaningful activity and relationships by supporting people in activities that are meaningful and enjoyable and that fit in with their lives, by involving people in the parts of the activity they can already do or almost do and by making the right thing to do obvious. It ensures success by providing just enough help and support. When people succeed, they experience the satisfaction and reinforcement of achievement and this increases the likelihood that they will get involved in the future. They also demonstrate their competence and just how much more they can do with the right support. The effect of this is to change how people view the individual they support or meet in the community and to increase the respect that people have for that individual. Once people start to experience these positive results of participating in activity, the likelihood of them taking part next time increases.

This motivational spiral is also true for staff – as they see the individuals they support gaining in skills and enjoying the activities in which they participate, staff too start to feel more confident and try new things with people. They feel more skilled, more valued and more respected by their peers and other people who see the results of their work. Other people involved with the individuals being supported – family, friends, neighbours, members of the public – will also experience the rewards of successful interactions and encounters.

Reducing difficulty
- respecting preferences and agendas
- selecting parts of task person can do
- making the right thing to do obvious

- more chance of getting involved
- more respect

Consequences
- increasing reinforcement
- demonstrating competence

Ensuring success
- providing just enough help to ensure success

Figure 3.3 The virtuous circle of active support

This virtuous circle implies a developmental perspective. Over time, people experiencing active support should learn that they are much more likely to succeed at new activities they try with support from staff. As they undertake activities with just enough help to succeed, they will often be in the *zone of proximal development* (Vygotsky 1978) – the area in which they can become more skilled as assistance is gradually withdrawn. For some people, the focus of assistance is likely to shift from how to do particular tasks to how to organise and plan them. Given a life full of opportunities and with skilled support at hand, there are also possibilities for using specific educational approaches (such as pairing more and less reinforcing activities, shaping successive approximations and varying patterns and schedules of reinforcement) specifically to increase skill development.

Even without specific educational input, and although the focus of active support is engagement rather than teaching, people receiving good active support would be expected to increase their skills over time. There is some evidence for this from research and this is described below.

Research on staff support of engagement in meaningful activity and relationships

Chapter 1 presented a broad account of the research on active support and the impact it has on engagement. Appendix 2 summarises the findings from all available published data and the analysis of some data currently being prepared for publication. This omits studies that were primarily about resettlement from institutions to community-based settings. In some of these studies, active support may have been part of the training for staff when they moved settings, but it is obviously not possible to separate the effect of introducing active support from the effect of moving out of an institution.

As well as observational measures of engagement and staff support minute by minute, some of these studies use a rating scale completed for each person by the observer on the basis of the whole observation period. This is the active support measure (Mansell and Elliott 1996), which is intended to include a wider range of aspects of support than the momentary time sample. It includes 15 items focusing on the opportunities for involvement and the skills with which staff provided and supported those opportunities, each scored on a scale of 0 (poor, inconsistent support/performance) to 3 (good, consistent support/performance). The items are:

- age-appropriateness of activities and materials
- 'real' rather than pretend or very simple activities
- choice of activities
- demands presented carefully
- tasks appropriately analysed to facilitate service-user involvement
- sufficient staff contact for service users
- graded assistance to ensure service-user success
- speech matches developmental level of service user
- interpersonal warmth
- differential reinforcement of adaptive behaviour
- staff notice and respond to service-user communication
- staff manage serious challenging behaviour well

- staff work as a coordinated team to support service users

- teaching is embedded in everyday activities

- written plans in routine use.

The maximum possible score is 45 and for each person a percentage score is calculated. In the data presented here, this percentage score was then averaged across individuals within each service to produce a service level score. A score of 67 per cent or more represents good, consistent active support. A score of 33 per cent or less represents no or very weak active support. A score between 33 per cent and 67 per cent represents mixed support.

The effect of active support on engagement in meaningful activity and relationships

Appendix 2 shows that where active support is implemented, it results in significant increases in engagement in meaningful activity. Where implementation was weak, there were smaller or no increases in engagement. For example, in the Hughes and Mansell (1992) study, the training in the initial services was not passed on to other services and there were difficulties creating incentives and motivation for staff. Although the services thought they were doing better, independent evaluation showed no change in engagement or contact from staff over time. In the Jones *et al.* (2001b) study, those in the third phase of the intervention, where managers were trained and then were responsible for training staff without further input from the training team, did not show significant increases in engagement or contact from staff. The critical element that appeared to be missing from this phase was hands-on training for staff.

Data from secondary analysis of the Ashman and Beadle-Brown (2006) data and the data drawn from Beadle-Brown *et al.* (2011) illustrates the effect of weak implementation. Although on average these studies show higher engagement levels (43% and 45% respectively) than the baseline data presented in Chapter 2 (38%), these are only very modest improvements (equivalent to just three or four minutes in each hour). When engagement is compared for people receiving good active support versus those receiving weak or mixed active support, there are much larger differences (Table 3.1). This applies to the whole sample but the difference is even more marked when people with adaptive behaviour scale (ABS) scores less than 181 are compared. These are people for whom, in some studies at least, active support is found to be most effective. Thus, in the Ashman and Beadle-Brown (2006) dataset, those receiving good active support were engaged for 19 minutes more in the hour than those receiving weak or mixed active support. In the Beadle-Brown *et al.* (2011) dataset, the equivalent figure is 17 minutes in each hour (see Tables 3.1 and 3.2). In both cases, the people receiving good active support had significantly higher scores on the adaptive behaviour scale, perhaps indicating that staff were finding it easier to provide good active support to them rather than to people with higher support needs, as well as that people with higher ABS scores could do more for themselves. Nevertheless, taking these results with the experimental studies already published, these data show that good active support produces dramatic results.

Further evidence that engagement is related to the implementation of active support is found in correlations between the active support measure and levels of engagement. Beadle-Brown, Hutchinson and Welton (2012) report a significant correlation between active support measure scores and levels of engagement (*rho*=0.504, $p<0.01$) and secondary analysis of the datasets reported by Ashman and Beadle-Brown (2006) and Beadle-Brown *et al.* (2011) found correlations of 0.662 ($p<0.001$) and 0.646 ($p<0.001$) respectively.

Examination of the changes in the active support measure in these data shows that improvements occur across almost all items of the scale. For example, Table 3.3 presents the changes on each item of the active support measure between baseline and after active support training for the Beadle-Brown *et al.* (2012) sample. A similar picture was found for the other datasets (Ashman and Beadle-Brown 2006; Beadle-Brown *et al.* 2011).

The other useful measure of implementation of active support is the amount of assistance to be engaged in meaningful activity that people are observed to receive from staff. As can be seen from Appendix 2, implementation of active support generally resulted in significant increases in the levels of assistance received from staff. Secondary analyses of some of these studies have shown that active support training increases the probability that assistance is followed by engagement (Felce *et al.* 2000; Smith *et al.* 2002; Stancliffe *et al.* 2008a).

Table 3.1 Engagement, assistance, contact and ABS score for the Ashman and Beadle-Brown (2006) sample for those receiving good active support and those receiving weak to mixed active support, both for the whole sample and for those with ABS scores less than 181

	Weak/mixed active support	Good active support	Statistical significance
Whole sample			
Number of people	168	149	
Mean ABS (range)	103 (29–223)	154 (31–98)	z = 7.951 p < 0.001
Mean ASM (range)	45 (10–66.66)	79 (66.67–100)	z = 14.41 p < 0.001
Mean engagement (range)	28 (0–100)	60 (0–100)	z = 10.26 p < 0.001
Mean assistance (range)	7 (0–43)	16 (0–64)	z = 6.08 p < 0.001
Mean other contact (range)	15 (0–80)	23 (0–80)	z = 4.33 p < 0.001
Sub sample with ABS scores less than 181			
Number of people	125	70	
Mean ABS (range)	89 (29–171)	115 (31–178)	z = 4.376 p < 0.001
Mean ASM (range)	42 (10–64)	79 (69–97)	z = 11.782 p < 0.001
Mean engagement (range)	23 (0–97)	54 (0–97)	z = 7.934 p < 0.001
Mean assistance (range)	7 (0–43)	19 (0–64)	z = 6.331 p < 0.001
Mean contact (range)	14 (0–80)	22 (0–73)	z = 3.144 p < 0.01

Table 3.2 Engagement, assistance, contact and ABS score for the Beadle-Brown *et al.* (2011) sample for those receiving good active support and those receiving weak to mixed active support, both for the whole sample and for those with ABS scores less than 181

	Weak/mixed active support	Good active support	Statistical significance
Whole sample			
Number of people	112	172	
Mean ABS (range)	81 (0–234)	147 (0–267)	z = 8.439 p < 0.001
Mean ASM (range)	41 (8–64)	85 (66.67–100)	z = 14.283 p < 0.001
Mean engagement (range)	24 (0–100)	58 (0–100)	z = 9.648 p < 0.001
Mean assistance (range)	6 (0–60)	12 (0–80)	z = 4.569 p < 0.001
Mean other contact (range)	17 (0–61)	25 (0–80)	z = 3.903 p < 0.001
Sub sample with ABS scores less than 181			
Number of people	102	98	
Mean ABS (range)	71 (0–166)	109 (0–177)	z = 5.840 p < 0.001
Mean ASM (range)	12 (8–64)	84 (69–100)	z = 12.311 p < 0.001
Mean engagement (range)	22 (0–100)	50 (0–100)	z = 7.431 p < 0.001
Mean assistance (range)	6 (0–60)	13 (0–80)	z = 5.362 p < 0.001
Mean contact (range)	17 (0–61)	25 (0–80)	z = 3.601 p < 0.001

The highest average level of assistance reported in the studies in Appendix 2 was 22 per cent in the first of the Andover houses (Felce, de Kock and Repp 1986), reflecting that each person was observed receiving assistance, on average, for over a fifth of the time. Very few studies have ever reached that level, on average, and most studies appear to achieve between 10 and 15 per cent assistance after training in active support (the second house in the Andover study achieved 14% assistance). Of course, these are average figures and some individuals in many of the studies do receive over 20 per cent assistance, and, as illustrated by some of the studies in Appendix 2, where active support was rated as good, average levels of assistance did reach levels of 16–18 per cent.

When engagement is compared for people receiving good versus weaker assistance (taking the 14% found in the second Andover house as the cut-off), a similar pattern is found to the comparison based on the active support measure. In the Ashman and Beadle-Brown (2006) dataset, those receiving good assistance were engaged for 11 minutes more in the hour than those receiving lower levels of assistance (see Table 3.4). A similar pattern was found for the Beadle-Brown *et al.* (2011) dataset (see Table 3.5). In both cases, there was no significant difference between the groups on the adaptive behaviour scale, strengthening the case that differences were due to the amount of assistance people were receiving.

Taking all the studies from Appendix 1 where both assistance and engagement data were available prior to or without full implementation of active support, the correlation between engagement and assistance (see Figure 3.4) was low (rho=0.345). That is, the extent to which people were engaged in meaningful activity and relationships depended on other things – probably on the opportunities available in the environment and the individual's support needs. However, in studies where active support had been implemented or training had been provided, the relationship between assistance and engagement (Figure 3.5) was stronger (rho=0.651).

Table 3.3 Mean and percentage scoring good (3) on each item of the active support measure at baseline (T1) and follow-up (T2) for the Beadle-Brown et al. (2011) dataset

Active support measure item	T1 mean	T2 mean	T1 % good	T2 % good	Significance z	p
Age-appropriateness of activities and materials	2.33	2.74	48.5	84	2.134	p < 0.05
'Real' rather than pretend or very simple activities	1.73	1.94	0	29	1.149	n.s.
Choice of activities	0.94	1.77	0	23	3.692	p < 0.001
Demands presented carefully	1	1.81	0	26	3.692	p < 0.001
Tasks appropriately analysed to facilitate service-user involvement	1.03	1.84	0	26	3.63	p < 0.001
Sufficient staff contact for service-users	0.82	2.03	0	26	4.604	p < 0.001
Graded assistance to ensure service-user success	0.39	1.77	0	26	4.665	p < 0.001
Speech matches developmental level of service-user	1.24	2	9	29	3.412	p < 0.01
Interpersonal warmth	2.09	2.9	30	94	3.447	p < 0.01
Differential reinforcement of adaptive behaviour	1.88	2.5	0	57	2.333	p < 0.05
Staff notice and respond to service user communication	1.24	2.55	9	58	4.409	p < 0.001
Staff manage serious challenging behaviour well	1	2.2	0	40	not enough cases	
Staff work as a coordinated team to support service-users	0.52	2	0	6	4.755	p < 0.001
Teaching is embedded in everyday activities	0	0.97	0	10	3.573	p < 0.001
Written plans in routine use	0	0	0	0	0	n.s.

Table 3.4 Engagement, assistance, contact and ABS score for the Ashman and Beadle-Brown (2006) sample for those receiving assistance 14 per cent and above of the time compared to those receiving assistance less than 14 per cent of the time, for the whole sample and for those with ABS scores less than 181

	Assistance <14%	Assistance 14% and above	Statistical significance
Whole sample			
Number of people	106	194	
Mean ABS (range)	124 (29–265)	129 (31–260)	z = 0.586 n.s.
Mean ASM (range)	54 (10–97)	72 (24–97)	z = 6.622 p < 0.001
Mean engagement (range)	36 (0–100)	54 (0–100)	z = 5.158 p < 0.001
Mean assistance (range)	4 (0–13)	25 (14–64)	z = 14.550 p < 0.001
Mean other contact (range)	17 (0–100)	22 (0–73)	z = 3.250 p < 0.01
Sub sample with ABS scores less than 181			
Number of people	147	78	
Mean ABS (range)	102 (29–180)	104 (31–178)	z = 0.387 n.s.
Mean ASM (range)	48 (10–90)	70 (24–97)	z = 7.131 p < 0.001
Mean engagement (range)	28 (0–100)	49 (0–97)	z = 5.706 p < 0.001
Mean assistance (range)	4 (0–13)	25(14–64)	z = 12.564 p < 0.001
Mean contact (range)	16 (0–100)	22 (0–73)	z = 2.984 p < 0.01

Table 3.5 Engagement, assistance, contact and ABS score for the Beadle-Brown *et al.* (2011) sample for those receiving good assistance (14% and over) and those receiving low assistance (<14%), both for the whole sample and for those with ABS scores less than 181

	Assistance <14%	Assistance 14% and above	Statistical significance
Whole sample			
Number of people	224	76	
Mean ABS (range)	120 (0–267)	121 (0–225)	z = 0.324 n.s.
Mean ASM (range)	64 (8–97)	79 (15–100)	z = 4.562 p < 0.001
Mean engagement (range)	39 (0–100)	57 (0–100)	z = 4.543 p < 0.001
Mean assistance (range)	4 (0–13)	26 (14–80)	z = 13.391 p < 0.001
Mean other contact (range)	19 (0–80)	29 (0–80)	z = 4.701 p < 0.001
Sub sample with ABS scores less than 181			
Number of people	158	58	
Mean ABS (range)	89 (0–180)	98 (0–177)	z = 1.944 n.s.
Mean ASM (range)	58 (8–97)	76 (15–100)	z = 5.209 p < 0.001
Mean engagement (range)	31 (0–100)	51 (0–100)	z = 5.409 p < 0.001
Mean assistance (range)	4 (0–13)	26 (14–80)	z = 11.522 p < 0.001
Mean contact (range)	19 (0–80)	27 (0–80)	z = 3.288 p < 0.01

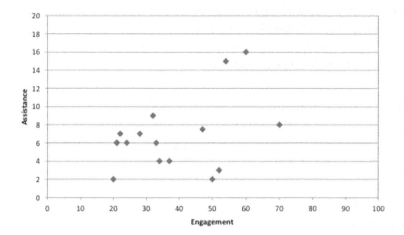

Figure 3.4 Relationship between engagement and assistance without the implementation of active support from studies reviewed across time

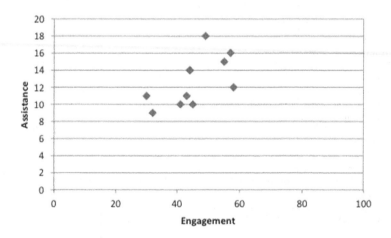

Figure 3.5 Relationship between engagement and assistance post active support from studies over time

Some of the individual studies reported in Appendix 2 also show this relationship. For example, Beadle-Brown *et al.* (2012) report a significant correlation between engagement and assistance at follow-up (*rho*=0.709, p<0.001, n=31). Analysis of the Ashman and Beadle-Brown (2006) dataset and the Beadle-Brown *et al.* (2011) dataset also produced significant but rather weaker correlations between engagement and assistance (rho=0.359 and 0.287 respectively). However, these samples included more able people, and if the analysis was repeated for people with more severe disabilities (that is, those with an ABS score less than 151), then rather stronger correlations were found (rho=0.478 and 0.476 respectively).

Overall, this is a compelling picture that active support improves engagement in meaningful activity and relationships by people with severe or profound intellectual disabilities. Where active support is properly implemented, it has clear results that are likely to make an important difference to the quality of life of the people served. Weak results appear often to be due to weak implementation.

The effect of adaptive behaviour on engagement in meaningful activity and relationships

The second explanation for weaker results than in the best studies is the level of support required by the individuals concerned. Jones *et al.* (2001b) found that people with an adaptive behaviour scale score of 181 or more experienced little benefit from active support. The likely explanation for this is that these people can engage in meaningful activity and relationships without help, as long as the opportunity presents itself. As long as there are opportunities for activity and relationships, and as long as people are not prevented from taking them, then people with low support needs should be able to engage successfully without much intervention from staff.

Tables 3.6 and 3.7 summarise the change in engagement across time or across group for studies where this information is available. Although too small a sample to explore statistically, it does appear that change in engagement was greater for samples where ABS scores were lower.

Table 3.6 Summary of change in engagement over time, from available pre- and post-intervention studies

Pre- and post-implementation study					
Paper	Engage-ment T1	Engage-ment T2	change	% change	ABS
Jones *et al.* (1999)	33	57	24	73	115
Jones *et al.* (2001a)	47	55	8	17	144
Jones *et al.* (2001b) Phase 1	42	53	11	26	129
Jones *et al.* (2001b) Phase 2	53	56	3	6	163
Jones *et al.* (2001b) Phase 3	58	57	-1	-2	170
Bradshaw *et al.* (2004)	17	26	9	53	94
Stancliffe *et al.* (2007)	42	54	12	29	More able sample
Beadle-Brown *et al.* (2012)	20	41	21	105	77

Table 3.7 Summary of differences in engagement between groups where active support has been implemented and those where it had not been implemented

Experimental/comparison studies								
Paper	Engagement No/weak AS	Engagement AS implementation	Difference	% difference	No/weak ASM assistance	AS implementation assistance	ABS no AS	ABS good AS
Ashman and Beadle-Brown (2006) whole group	28	60	32	114	7	16	103	154
Ashman and Beadle-Brown (2006) severe group	22	49	27	123	7	18	83	103
Mansell et al. (2008)	70	77	7	10	8	12	173	182
Beadle-Brown et al. (2012)	24	58	34	142	6	12	81	147
Beadle-Brown et al. (in press) severe group	21	44	23	110	6	14	69	91

However, not all studies have found this effect. Stancliffe *et al.* (2007) found no systematic difference in the effect of active support on people with differing levels of adaptive behaviour. The amount of change may also be relevant. In the Jones *et al.* (2001a, 2001b) studies, the increases in engagement were relatively small. Table 3.8 summarises the findings from the Jones *et al.* studies (with more detail in Appendix 2) and illustrates that in the earlier study (Jones *et al.* 1999) the amount of change in assistance and engagement was greater than in the 2001a and 2001b studies. One possible reason for this may have been the level of ability of the group – the group that showed the greatest increase was the more severely disabled group. Mean scores on the Aberrant Behaviour Checklist (ABC) (Aman *et al.* 1985) were similar across all three studies, ruling out challenging behaviour as a contributing factor.

Table 3.8 Summary of changes in assistance and engagement in the Jones *et al.* 1999 and 2001 papers

	Jones *et al.* 1999		Jones *et al.* 2001a		Jones *et al.* 2001b (Phase 1 sample)	
	Pre	Post	Pre	Post	Pre	Post
Assistance (% of time)	6	16	8	15	Verbal: 6.8 Non-verbal: 2.8	Verbal: 14.1 Non-verbal: 12.3
Engagement (% of time)	33	57	47	55	42	54
Average ABS score	115		144		129	

Secondary analysis of the data from Ashman and Beadle-Brown (2006) shows differences between those receiving good active support and those receiving weak or mixed active support both below and above the ABS 181 threshold (see Table 3.1 above). For those people with ABS scores less than 181 (n=195), there were significant differences between those receiving good active support and those receiving weak or mixed active support for total engagement, non-social activity, assistance, other contact from staff and social activity.

However, for the 60 people with ABS scores of 181 and above, there were also significant differences between the two groups. Those receiving good active support (n=51) spent more time engaged (mean 75%, range 8–100) than those receiving weak or mixed active support (mean 49%, range 20–73). This was statistically significant ($z=3.305$ $p<0.01$), although should be treated somewhat cautiously given the small number of people not rated as receiving good active support in this instance. In terms of staff support, assistance and other contact from staff were also significantly higher for those receiving good active support ($z=2.760$ $p<0.01$ and $z=2.106$ $p<0.05$ respectively).

Where people with lower support needs are also benefiting from active support including higher levels of assistance, this may reflect that the tasks they are doing are more complex. For example, people may not need help from staff to go to the shop, pick items off the shelves, pay for them and carry them home, but they may need help to plan their purchases and budget for them, or to understand the timetable for public transport. Helping people do this through graded assistance is as much active support as other kinds of help and should result both in higher levels of engagement and also in more complex activities.

The potential for a better quality of life

The wide range of levels of support needed among people with severe or profound intellectual disabilities is reflected in the level of engagement in meaningful activity and relationships that it is possible for people to achieve. Good active support compensates, at least to some extent, for the level of disability and enables people to do more than would otherwise be the case. Secondary analysis of the available datasets was undertaken to identify the levels of engagement that it is possible to achieve when good active support (ASM score of 67% and above) is provided for individuals of different levels of ability. This analysis is summarised in Table 3.9 below.

These results show that people with lower support needs achieve higher levels of engagement when provided with good active support. Taken at face value, these seem logical results. The person with profound intellectual and multiple disabilities is less likely to be able to sustain the energy and attention, and less likely to have the skills and abilities required, to engage as much as the person with much less severe disabilities. However, the most important results in Table 3.9 are the upper ends of the ranges reported. These show that even people needing the highest levels of support can engage in meaningful activities and relationships at a level comparable to the average achieved by much less severely disabled people. Similarly, the ranges shown for assistance indicate that some individuals are receiving high levels of assistance – much higher than the averages reported in group studies.

A further indication of the potential of good active support to improve people's lives is the 'added value' effect of increasing assistance. Mansell (1995) showed that engagement levels in a group of people receiving an early form of active support after moving out of institutions increased beyond the level of assistance provided. Similarly, Beadle-Brown et al. (2012) showed that among a group of people receiving increased assistance, an increase of 12 per cent assistance on average resulted in people spending 22 per cent more of the time engaged in meaningful activity and relationships.

Impact of active support on other domains

Although active support has mainly been studied for its effect on engagement in meaningful activity and relationships, focusing on the extent of participation in activity and in social behaviour, some studies have sought to measure other aspects of quality of life. Thus, active support has also been shown to increase people's participation in different daily living activities (Beadle-Brown et al., 2012; Jones et al. 2001a; Stancliffe et al. 2007), in social and community activities (Jones et al. 2001a; Stancliffe et al. 2007), as well as increasing people's skills and adaptive behaviour (Beadle-Brown et al., 2012; Felce et al. 1986; Mansell et al. 2002b; Mansell, McGill and Emerson 2001; Stancliffe et al. 2010).

Although active support is an important element of positive behaviour support (see Chapter 7), very little research has shown a significant decrease in challenging behaviour following the successful implementation of active support. Both Smith et al. (2002) and Jones et al. (2001b) reported no change in challenging behaviour after active support training. Bradshaw et al. (2004) reported some increases in challenging behaviour after training. However, recent research by Koritsas *et al.* (2008) and Stancliffe *et al.* (2010) have both found evidence of a significant decrease in at least some types of challenging behaviour and, in the case of the Koritsas *et al.* study, in Total Behavior Problem Score on the Developmental Behaviour Checklist for Adults (Einfeld, Tonge and Mohr 2003). Beadle-Brown *et al.* (2012) found that there was a significant decrease in scores on the stereotypical domain of the ABC and over half of the people included in the study showed lower scores overall on the ABC. They also reported that there was a significant decrease in the number of behaviours rated as severe. Of the seven people rated as showing five or more severe behaviours at baseline, only one was rated as doing so at follow-up, though this was not statistically significant due to the small numbers.

Active support also places emphasis on offering and supporting choice-making opportunities for people. However, very few studies have examined the impact of active support on choice-making opportunities or support. Stancliffe *et al.* (2007, 2010) explored some of the indirect effects of implementing active support (in addition to the direct effect on engagement levels) and found that there was a slight but non-significant decrease in depression and slight but non-significant increase in adaptive behaviour following the introduction of active support. There was no change in choice, challenging behaviour or contact with family and friends. In contrast, Beadle-Brown *et al.* (2012) found that opportunities for choice, as rated by staff, increased significantly with the introduction of active support and observed choice during activities was also significantly higher.

Conclusion

Chapter 2 showed that engagement in meaningful activity and relationships was an important indicator of quality of life, that it was typically much lower for people with severe or profound intellectual disabilities than for the general population and that severity of disability was associated with poorer outcomes. Although severity of disability appeared to be very important, environmental factors also appeared to influence engagement. In this chapter, we have explored this, describing 'the enabling relationship' as the fundamental component of active support.

Table 3.9 Levels of engagement and assistance when active support is rated as good (percentage scores above 66.66%)

Study/dataset	Variable	ABS groups						
		ABS 0–30	ABS 31–60	ABS 61–90	ABS 91–120	ABS 121–150	ABS 151–180	ABS 181+
Ashman and Beadle-Brown (2006) dataset	Mean (range) engagement		43 (15–60)	37 (15–64)	52 (16–93)	61 (22–95)	69 (29–97)	75 (8–100)
	Mean (range) assistance		23 (8–35)	25 (0–60)	19 (0–53)	17 (0–64)	18 (0–53)	14 (0–54)
	Mean (range) ABS		37 (31–50)	78 (64–86)	101 (93–114)	136 (121–149)	165 (154–178)	213 (182–265)
	Mean (range) ASM		74 (69–81)	82 (69–93)	78 (69–95)	80 (69–97)	79 (69–95)	83 (69–97)
	n		7	11	14	18	17	51
Beadle-Brown et al. (2011) dataset	Mean (range) engagement	30 (12–56)	32 (6–70)	39 (7–80)	41 (7–80)	61 (13–100)	64 (0–100)	71 (6–100)
	Mean (range) assistance	14 (3–22)	12 (0–40)	15 (0–40)	11 (0–27)	17 (0–80)	11 (0–35)	9 (0–50)
	Mean (range) ABS	10 (0–29)	43 (31–60)	73 (62–86)	104 (95–116)	134 (121–149)	165 (152–267)	211 (182–267)
	Mean (range) ASM	75 (71–77)	79 (69–90)	82 (71–97)	85 (72–100)	86 (69–97)	86 (69–100)	88 (69–100)
	n	3	13	17	18	22	22	63

Study	Measure						
Mansell et al. (2011)	Mean (range) engagement	70			89 (82–95)	54 (20–88)	61 (0–100)
	Mean (range) assistance	15			11 (5–18)	0	2 (0–20)
	Mean (range) ABS	48			141 (135–147)	157 (157–159)	217 (185–253)
	Mean (range) ASM	79			85 (85–85)	97 (97–97)	85 (69–98)
	n	1			2	2	14
Beadle-Brown et al. (2012)	Mean (range) engagement		62 (43–81)	44 (22–67)	82	65 (39–81)	
	Mean (range) assistance		16 (9–23)	14 (4–24)	47	16 (6–27)	
	Mean (range) ABS		75 (67–83)	108 (107–109)	145	162 (154–171)	
	Mean (range) ASM		83 (79–87)	78 (78–79)	81	86 (81–91)	
	n		2	2	1	2	

Research on active support has generally focused on quantitative indicators such as the active support measure and observed assistance, and their effect on engagement in meaningful activity and relationships. There are some qualitative descriptions of stronger and weaker active support (Clement and Bigby 2010; Felce and Toogood 1988) but generally exploration of some of the broader aspects of the enabling relationship would be useful. There is also, as yet, very little research in settings other than group homes.

Notwithstanding these limitations, and especially when compared with the sparse evidence base for some other recent innovations (see Chapter 7), the available research provides an impressive body of evidence demonstrating that active support is effective at enabling people to engage in meaningful activity and relationships. For people with higher support needs, the effect of active support is to compensate for this so that people are able to engage at similar levels to people with less severe disabilities. Even for these people, active support can help improve people's engagement, either by giving people the freedom to do things they already have the skill to do (where they do not need much assistance) or by extending the range of available activities to more complex, more interesting and more demanding things, where the assistance needed is more to do with planning and organising than doing the task.

The gap between weaker and stronger implementation of active support is also striking in the research. Active support needs to be provided well to have a worthwhile impact on quality of life. Its success therefore depends on the quality of its implementation. Although each person providing support to an individual with severe or profound intellectual disabilities can try to build an enabling relationship, success is likely to depend on teamwork, organisation and leadership, often in a service-providing organisation. The rest of this book addresses these issues, starting with the organisation of staff teams.

CHAPTER 4

Organising Staff Support

The previous chapter described how those providing support to individuals with severe or profound intellectual disabilities could enable them to engage in meaningful activity and relationships. This 'enabling relationship' is the core of active support and, in principle, anyone providing support could choose to work in this way. However, an individual will usually be supported by more than one person, working as a team. In this situation, the team has to ensure that the support it provides is sufficiently consistent to be helpful. Sometimes, several people will be together receiving support – for example, people living together or at work or college together or meeting up on a social occasion. In these situations, support has to be organised so that individuals get the help they need, when they need it. The team has to coordinate itself to share out its members' time in a way that maximises people's control and engagement.

Organising staff support is therefore important if people are to be enabled to participate in activities and relationships. Many services attempt to organise staff support through the use of written guidance such as plans, protocols and monitoring forms. As explained in Chapter 1, our experience is that often these have become an end in themselves, instead of a means to achieving better active support. Although they are useful when used properly, they are not a substitute for good teamwork and practice leadership.

The first part of this chapter focuses on consistency and predictability of support, explaining why these are important and how staff can work together to achieve them. It then discusses the coordination of support in group situations and how staff can best organise themselves to provide the support people need. This is followed by a description of the kinds of plans, protocols and records that are being used to help staff organise themselves. Finally, the chapter concludes with a discussion of teamwork as an introduction to the topic of practice leadership in Chapter 5.

Increasing consistency and predictability of support

The first reason that a consistent way of providing support is important is simply that it respects the comfort and convenience of the person being supported. It recognises that everyone has preferences for how things are done, and that in this situation it is the preferences of the person being supported that should hold most sway over what members of the support team do. How could support be *person-centred* if it did not respect individual preferences? This respect extends to cultural, religious and family preferences. However unfamiliar or unimportant these might seem to staff providing support, respecting them is a fundamental expectation of civil relations.

Consistency may be particularly important for other reasons. Individuals who need to be able to predict accurately what is going to happen, perhaps because of autistic spectrum conditions, need consistent support to reassure them that events are going to unfold in the way they expect. Support provided in different ways will increase their anxiety and may make it more difficult for people to take part in the activity. Failure to provide support in a consistent way may also cause challenging behaviour – for example, because people become so anxious or upset that they use challenging behaviour to terminate the activity, or because some staff inadvertently provide support in a way that is known to trigger challenging behaviour.

Ashman *et al.* (2010) point out that the amount of consistency a person needs will vary; some people will be able to cope with more variety in how they are helped than will others. The goal is not, therefore, to iron out every little variation in the way activities are undertaken or how people are helped to do them, so that everyone is imprisoned in a rigid, unchanging prescription. On the other hand, whilst it might be important to try to support people to be able to cope with some changes and flexibility, this needs to be done in a planned way that respects the needs and wishes of the individual – having no structure or routine, or exposing people to lots of unplanned or unexpected changes in routine in order to 'teach' them to be flexible, is neither ethical nor effective. Instead, the goal is to respect people's own preferences, including their preferences for or tolerance of variety, to enable them to engage in the activities and relationships that make up their lives.

Consistency is, of course, experienced by the *individual* being supported. If a group of people live or work together, there is no suggestion that they should all receive support in the same way. This is one of the reasons why people are best supported individually or in small groups. If two people are supported by a team of six different staff, then 12 possible ways of doing things have to be considered and each member of staff has to remember two different approaches; if ten people are supported by a team of 30 different members of staff, then there are potentially 300 different ways of doing things and each member of staff has to remember ten different ways.

Training in active support emphasises achieving consistency through everyone recognising its importance and discussing and agreeing the best approach to support individuals to undertake an activity in the way they want. It is important to recognise that coming to this kind of agreement is not necessarily straightforward, for two main reasons:

- The way people do different tasks or activities is often value-laden. They do things a certain way because they believe that this is the 'right' way to do them – perhaps because they think the results are better, or perhaps because they think that the results reflect in some way on them.

- The participants in the discussion – people being supported and the members of the team supporting them – are not equal. Those being supported might expect that their preferences would prevail. But among the support team, differences in age, experience and culture are likely to lead some people to believe that their views should hold sway.

This means that the debate about how to support someone to do a task is 'loaded' and therefore more difficult to conduct and resolve. It requires good teamwork and good leadership to recognise that supporting someone in one way does not mean that people who would do things differently are bad, foolish or lazy. Members of the support team should be proud that they are able to set aside their own preferences in order to provide consistent help to the person they are supporting.

Making sure people get the support they need when they need it

When more than one person is being supported at a time, staff have to share out the support they provide to maximise participation and activity. By far the most common approach teams seem to have in this situation is to try to allocate one team member to each individual they are supporting. This 'one-to-one' allocation system has the advantage that the person providing support just has to focus on the one individual he or she is supporting. But in a situation where there is not enough support to give everyone his or her own support worker or personal assistant all the time, where one person has to provide support to two or three people, it also has some disadvantages.

If one team member is allocated to support two or three people, this limits the kind of activities each can do (they have to be in the same place, for example) and it also means that they are likely to have to wait before moving from one activity to the next, so that other people can get the support they need. In the research literature, this was first studied by LeLaurin and Risley (1972) in an infant day care centre. They showed that if a childcare worker was allocated to a group of children, then as children finished an activity they had to wait until the last child in the group had finished before the whole group would move to the next activity. Thus some of the time had to be spent disengaged, waiting. In the alternative (which they called 'zone' allocation), staff were allocated not to groups of children but to areas where activities took place. This meant that as children were ready, they could move to the next activity where there would be a member of staff who could help them get started. Children spent more time engaged in meaningful activity under these arrangements.

The same options often apply in supporting people with severe and profound intellectual disabilities. For example, if four people are supported by two staff at a mealtime, each member of staff could be allocated to support two individuals. This could easily mean that everyone would have to wait until the last person had finished their meal before moving on to whatever they were doing next. Although it might be possible to engage everyone in conversation and the meal until everyone had finished, it might not. The alternative would be that at some point in the meal one of the staff would go into the kitchen, so that as people wanted to leave the dining table, they could clear away their crockery and cutlery with support in the kitchen as well as the dining room. As the last people finished, the member of staff in the dining room could go to set up whatever the next activity was so that people leaving the kitchen could be supported when they arrived.

Allocating staff to areas or activities can, in this way, provide more support for people to engage in meaningful activity. Mansell *et al.* (2005) give another example to illustrate how to work like this. This approach does require good teamwork and coordination from staff, because they have to have worked out the flow of activities and the support needed for each of them over the coming period and they have to be mindful of this plan as events unfold. One way to think of this is that the people providing support, like the pilot of an aeroplane, need to have a 'flight plan'. They need to have a plan of what the people they are supporting are going to do over the coming period (such as the shift) and how as a team they are going to share out their support to enable everyone to get the help he or she needs, reducing to a minimum the amount of time people are kept waiting.

This cannot be a plan to be followed rigidly. Events may mean that the plan doesn't quite work out in practice – just as the pilot's flight plan might need to be modified. The point is that everyone will share the same sense of the pattern and sequence of activities, making it easier to adjust arrangements as circumstances dictate.

The way in which staff were helped to develop this idea of a shared plan of support in the Andover project was that they came on shift 15–30 minutes before the previous staff left and they used this time to discuss and develop a 'shift plan' (Mansell *et al.* 1987b, p.213 *et seq.*). A written plan was produced as an aide-memoire but the key point was that staff had thought through how they were going to provide the support needed – the product was their shared understanding, not a piece of paper. Examples of and suggestions for shift plans are given in the training materials available (Ashman *et al.* 2010; Jones *et al.* 1996a; Mansell *et al.* 2005).

Plans, protocols and paperwork

This brings us to the question of what kind of written plans and records are helpful in organising a team to provide active support. The previous chapter described how one of the essential components of active support is analysing the flow of activity to spot opportunities for the person being supported to take part. Thinking this through for a particular individual and a particular activity is helpful preparation and essential if a team of people have to be coordinated to provide consistent support. It can be written as a 'support plan' or an 'activity protocol', to provide a clear description of how best to support someone in a particular activity. Similarly, a team of people supporting more than one individual need to plan how to share out their support and this can be written as a 'shift plan' to provide an aide-memoire.

Support plans and shift plans are job-aids: that is, they are intended to help staff organise and conduct themselves in the right way by reminding them of or cueing them into providing the kind of support needed. Ashman *et al.* (2010) and Clement and Bigby (2010) suggest that written plans can provide a useful way of helping a new member of the support team, or a casual or relief member of staff, learn how to provide support in an otherwise unfamiliar situation. Ashman *et al.* recommend the 'unfamiliar competent worker' test: 'Could a reasonably competent support worker who has never worked here before use this shift plan to support people effectively for this shift?' (Ashman *et al.* 2010, p.63). Clement and Bigby (2010, p.153) make the point that written plans may be especially helpful for a new or less experienced staff team which is not yet practised at providing the support needed. Stancliffe *et al.* (2008b) also suggest that written records may signal to staff that the activity to which they refer is important, in an organisation where written material denotes importance.

These are all plausible arguments for writing plans. However, it is important to note that a deeper understanding of what needs to be done and why is likely to come from the discussion the team has to generate the plan rather than from just reading it. It seems unlikely that any plan could be so clearly set out, so detailed yet succinct enough to be easily digested, that it alone would be a useful guide to providing the support a person needs. It is the discussion – the thinking through the issues and developing a shared understanding among the support team – that is likely to be the most useful form of help. Reviewing and reflecting on how support is being provided in practice, in a discussion with other team members, can provide the opportunity for new staff to develop a fuller understanding of what they should be doing and why.

Rather similar concerns apply to recording the extent to which the individual takes part in activities. In the Andover demonstration project, a simple record of each person's participation in different activities was used (Mansell *et al.* 1987b, p.217 *et seq.*) and this was continued in the early training materials (Brown *et al.* 1987; Jones *et al.* 1996a). The purpose of this record was to help staff check that the individual they supported was successfully involved in a sufficiently wide range of activities and opportunities and was not 'stuck in a rut' of always doing the same thing. The record was a prompt for discussion in the staff meeting – it was the discussion that was the important thing.

Although the paperwork is just there as a prompt for thinking, discussion and problem solving, in our experience it is often treated as the important product. So we have seen examples where the production of paper is the end in itself:

- Staff teams who have devoted hours to writing a support plan for every conceivable activity for every individual they support so that they have a library of dozens of support plans, but where visiting shows that staff are not supporting people to engage in meaningful activity.

- Shift plans that are based around staff activities (which jobs staff have to do) rather than the people they support or that outline the activities for the people they support but do not actually record which staff will be supporting each activity.

- Services where the staff team has devised a detailed timetable spelling out what each person they support will be doing every quarter-hour during the waking day, providing a completely prescribed, rigid timetable that could not reflect choice and control by the individual. Perhaps fortunately, these timetables seem only designed to decorate a wall in an office, never actually to be implemented.

- Staff members sitting alone with a set of 'Keeping Track' forms (Brown *et al.* 1987), ticking boxes to say which activities people had or had not done, while the people they are supposed to be supporting sit disengaged in another part of the house.

Clement and Bigby (2010, p.144 *et seq.*) describe similar problems in the group homes that they studied, and McCubbery and Fyffe (2006) found that issues related to paperwork were a common problem in implementing active support in their study of implementation in Victoria. In a small-scale pilot study of 29 staff and managers supporting 22 people with severe and profound intellectual disabilities in England, Higgins (2010) found no correlation between paper-based records completed by support staff and engagement or support directly observed by the researcher.

These problems are not, of course, confined to the paperwork associated with active support. The filing cabinets of many service providers are stuffed with assessments, person-centred plans, incident reports and monitoring records that bear only the slightest relationship to what actually happens in the lives of people with intellectual disabilities. Even in respect of medication, where recording is most heavily regulated, nearly 40 per cent of care homes for younger adults in England surveyed by the Commission for Social Care Inspection (2006) did not meet national minimum standards and failures of record keeping were one of the three main deficits noted.

There seem to be several possible reasons why paperwork becomes an end in itself. Clement and Bigby (2010, p.149) point out that good plans and records require a standard of English literacy that many staff do not possess. They quote Fryer (2006) who estimates that 400,000 health and social care staff in England have literacy skills comparable to those of children leaving primary school. Poorly written plans or records may be less use as a primer for discussion and decision making but may be enough to satisfy management and regulators who give them only a cursory examination.

Having the discussion at the beginning of a shift with the people being supported and with colleagues to decide how to allocate support, or reviewing how well support is enabling people to undertake activities and sustain relationships, itself requires a degree of teamwork and skill in managing interaction that may be lacking. Bigby *et al.* (in press) describe how staff goals in group homes are sometimes not aligned with each other nor with the service aims and how this hinders good support. If plans and records are not forming the basis for regular discussion and problem solving (however well or badly they are written), then staff may not see them as important or may see them as only important to managers and regulators.

That staff believe that managers value paperwork is supported by a study by Mansell and Elliott (2001). They undertook in-depth interviews with 143 staff members in 35 group homes and three institution wards in England. Staff were given scenarios describing different tasks they might carry out and asked what would happen if they did, or failed to do, them (that is, who would notice, what would their reaction be). Whereas 76 per cent of staff said that there would be strong negative consequences for them from managers if they failed to do administrative tasks, only 62 per cent thought the same would be true if they failed to enable the people they were supporting to take part in activity. The same gradient was found for strong positive consequences from managers if staff did the tasks. Thus staff who give priority to administration may be responding to the contingencies established by their managers. If managers (or regulators) act as if the paperwork is what they care about, then it is perhaps not at all surprising that paperwork is what they get.

Mansell and Elliott's study also suggested that at least some staff found administration intrinsically more rewarding than working with the people they were supposed to be supporting. Staff sometimes said that whether or not there would be consequences from other people for their work, they would feel good or bad about it. The task that most staff members said would matter to them was administration, producing both positive and negative consequences when staff members did it. The interview transcripts show that this reflected both the sense of achievement that staff members had from completing administrative work and their concern that it took them away from the people they supported.

Written plans and records do have a part to play in helping staff provide support in the best way, both as a prompt or cue to do the right thing and as the basis for discussion and review. However, our experience is that there is such a great risk of written plans and records being seen as an end in themselves that they should not be relied upon as evidence of anything other than writing. Thus, we think it is essential in research on active support to include measurement of engagement in meaningful activity and relationships and the quality of support actually provided by staff, and not to rely on paper records as evidence of successful implementation. Similarly, managers, regulators and everyone concerned about the quality of life of individuals should look directly at engagement and support and not rely on paper records.

Working as a team

It is evident from the discussion above that teamwork is an important issue in organising staff to provide active support. There is extensive published research on teamwork and it is beyond the scope of this book to provide a comprehensive description. It is possible, however, to identify some key points that are particularly relevant to active support.

First, what kind of team are we talking about? Much of the research is on multi-professional teams, where each individual makes a distinct contribution to the team's work. This is not the case in services providing direct support to people with intellectual disabilities. Here the priority is that team members provide consistent, well-organised support to the individuals they serve. Each team member needs to be able to work in the same way as colleagues, and team members need to be able to substitute for each other without damaging the quality of support they provide. Thus, the research on the different and complementary roles that people might play in a team (for example, Belbin 1997) is less relevant here.[1] Nor are these 'task-and-finish' teams which have a relatively short life, defined by completing a particular piece of work. Ideally, teams should be sufficiently stable to provide good support that is closely tailored to individual needs in spite of changing circumstances over time, including changing

---

1   In the first Andover house (Mansell *et al.* 1987b), staff at an early team meeting commented that among them the older women with more experience of raising their own families were better at cooking and cleaning than the younger members of the team, whose strengths were in helping people learn new skills. The obvious suggestion was made that the older women should do most of the cooking and cleaning while the younger members did most of the work focused on enabling independence. After discussion, though, the team decided the opposite – that the younger members should do more cooking and cleaning and the older members more support for independence so that everyone developed a high level of competence at supporting people in all the activities they did.

membership as new staff join and others leave. This means that research on the formation of teams and the stages they go through (such as the popular 'forming–storming–norming–performing' model of Tuckman (1965)) is also less relevant.

A team is more than a group of people – above all, it is a group with a purpose. People working together to provide the support an individual needs and wants must have shared goals, a shared vision of what they are trying to achieve and a shared sense of direction. More than this, a team providing support needs to share the methods used, so that everyone's approach is consistent. This implies the development of norms – shared rules about the way the team works to which all its members subscribe. These norms will be about two broad areas (Morgan, Salas and Glickman 1994). First, there will be norms about the tasks that team members perform – how they provide support to the individuals they serve and their use of plans, protocols and records. In addition, there will be norms about the way team members work together – the interaction they have with each other, their relationships, reciprocity, coordination and cooperation. Together, these form what is often called the informal culture of the staff group.

Social identity theory research (Tajfel and Turner 1986) shows that as soon as people begin to distinguish themselves as a group they start to develop shared views about what makes them distinct from and better than others. This process continues as the group develops and includes the development of norms about behaviour and characteristics of group members which are then defended and maintained by the group as new members join, through a process of socialisation. This is a powerful and apparently universal social process which happens whether we like it or not. The question therefore becomes 'What norms or rules does the support team develop?'

Unfortunately, there is plenty of evidence that the norms or rules developed by teams of staff supporting people with intellectual disabilities are often incompatible with the achievement of a good quality of life for the people they serve. There is a large literature describing how staff in institutions for people with intellectual disabilities developed institutional care practices (Jones *et al.* 1975; King, Raynes and Tizard 1971; Morris 1969) which became habitual, ingrained ways of working. The same problems have been found in more modern services. Cambridge (1999) describes how a team of staff in a group home developed a set of rules about responding to challenging behaviour designed to intimidate the people living there into submission, and how new staff were then cajoled and bullied into adopting this approach. A very similar picture was portrayed in the television programme *Undercover Care: The Abuse Exposed* (British Broadcasting Corporation 2011), in which a team of non-professional direct care staff had developed abusive care practices which they actively discussed, agreed and taught to new staff, apparently unnoticed or tolerated by their managers and the inspectors visiting the service.

Although these examples are about abuse and assault, the development of anti-therapeutic norms is documented more widely. Bigby *et al.* (in press) reanalysed data from a large study of the replacement of an institution in Victoria with group homes (Bigby, Cooper and Reid 2010) and identified five dimensions of staff subculture that characterised under-performing services. These were:

- misalignment of power-holder values with the service organisation's espoused values, characterised by staff saying 'We're not going to do it that way'

- seeing the people served by the team as essentially different ('Not like us')

- defining their role as doing for rather than doing with ('We look after them')

- a focus on staff goals, agendas and needs rather than those of the people served ('Get it done so we can sit down')

- resistance to ideas from the wider organisation and prevarication about improvement ('Yes, but').

The problem here is that the relatively high degree of autonomy experienced by staff supporting people with intellectual disabilities can be misused. It is a problem recognised in the general management literature:

> The overall risk with autonomous work groups is that they will come to set norms and objectives that do not match those of the organisation...although the reported studies

always describe studies where there is a synchronization of group and organisation goals, there is clearly a possibility that the groups might misappropriate the trust and relaxation of control. (Handy 1985, pp.333–4)

The implication of this is that the process of team building – the development of the norms and rules that will guide their action – cannot be left to chance. It needs to be actively nurtured and managed in the direction of the overall philosophy of providing good services. The characteristics of this supportive team culture would include the opposites of those found by Bigby *et al.* (in press):

- alignment of power-holder values with the service organisation's espoused values, so that staff readily express commitment to those values and have a full understanding of them and their implications for action

- seeing the people served by the team as essentially the same as other people, with the same sorts of needs and aspirations and the same claim on respect, time and effort as anyone else

- defining their role as enabling people to grow in independence, participation and control, to the greatest extent possible

- focusing on the goals, agendas and needs of the people served rather than on their own

- being open to ideas from the wider organisation and willing to keep trying to improve the support they provide.

Cherniss, writing about the effect of the normative structure of services on staff burnout, describes successful services:

in which most staff enthusiastically supported and used the program's treatment philosophy. In these programs, the treatment philosophy was frequently referred to and used by staff in both formal meetings and informal discussion. They would engage in animated debates about what the guiding philosophy required in a particular case…the staff seemed to be engaged in constant elaboration and revision of the model, based on their clinical experience with it… when that treatment philosophy 'comes alive' for staff and

becomes a central part of their thinking [can] it help sustain
hope and involvement. (1980, pp.103–4)

If that is the goal, how can it be achieved?

The first and most basic requirement prerequisite for this kind
of teamwork is that members of the team have to meet each other in
order to discuss, develop and review their approach. If services are
designed to deliver support to people in a completely fragmented
way, in which very large numbers of different individuals are paid to
deliver short (for example, 15-minute) periods of support throughout
the week, it will not be possible to develop good team working. Since
this appears to be the norm in old people's domiciliary services in the
UK, for example (Commission for Social Care Inspection 2005), it is
important to recognise and resist it where it is proposed. Finding time
for staff to develop a shared ethos of work together seems likely to
be an important contribution to good-quality support. If it is difficult
to organise, because of problems of geography, then virtual meetings
such as video-conferencing may be tried, perhaps as part of an overall
strategy to build a strong sense of cohesion and purpose across the
wider organisation.

Team members not only have to be able to meet together to develop
a shared approach, but they also have to have the opportunity to work
alongside more experienced colleagues who can help them develop
and improve their practice. This means seeing support provided well
by a more experienced and skilled co-worker but also working with
someone who can give feedback about how to improve, who can act
as a mentor or practice leader and who can enable the less experienced
team member to succeed. Of course, the person supported will also be
providing feedback, but for many people with severe and profound
intellectual disabilities this will be limited and may not be enough on
its own to sustain good practice.

The opportunity to work alongside good team members is
important not just for the practical support skills they have but
for the way the philosophy and values of the team are shaped and
maintained. If the less experienced team member says that the person
he or she is supporting wants to do some ironing but he or she would
prefer to watch a video, the more experienced team member should
be explaining why the ironing is what will happen and ensuring that
it happens well. The role modelling provided by experienced team

members extends to the language used and the values and norms it betrays.

Thus, it is clear that leadership plays a strong role in creating an effective team properly focused on providing good support. In their study of underperforming group homes set up to replace an institution in Victoria, Bigby *et al.* (in press) give examples of teams where there is no leadership at all (so every member of staff does what they want) or where the power in the team is held by a small group that may not even include the team leader. Where this happens, it is difficult to see how the necessary degree and quality of teamwork, focused on the goals of supporting the people served, can be achieved. Good leadership of the support team seems critical, not just at the outset but in facing the continuing challenge to keep on the right track, to incorporate new people as they arrive and to see off external challenges to providing good support.

Conclusion

The reality is that there is usually more than one person providing support to an individual with severe or profound intellectual disabilities, sometimes in a situation where support is being provided to several individuals. This means that the people providing support have to be coordinated. Coordination is required both to deliver consistent support in the best form for the individual and to ensure that support is provided when people need it.

Although written plans and protocols might be a useful prompt to team members as to how to organise themselves and how to provide support, they are unlikely to be sufficient. More important is the thinking and discussion between team members (and the person they are supporting, his or her advocates and family) about how best to provide the support the person needs and wants. This is likely to provide a deeper understanding than following a list of instructions.

Thus, good teamwork is the key to providing well-organised, consistent support. This involves the development of a shared vision of the goals of the team and also a shared philosophy of how team members provide support. It is maintained by norms or rules which provide team members with expectations about what they should do and support and reinforcement for doing it.

The development of a good team approach cannot, however, be left to chance. Given the evidence that teams providing support to people with severe and profound intellectual disabilities often develop inappropriate, anti-therapeutic norms, the process of team building and management requires leadership. This places the team leader in a particularly important position both as a source of technical knowledge and skill to provide the right kind of support and as someone who can facilitate the development of a strong team committed to the right things and ensure that this is maintained over time. This is the role we have called 'practice leadership' and it is the subject of the next chapter.

CHAPTER 5

Practice Leadership

Introduction

Chapter 4 concluded with the point that in order to ensure that staff work together as an effective team, good leadership is required. Given that the people providing support need to work consistently and to the agenda of the individuals they serve, team leaders need to be able to support the development of staff knowledge and skills and to provide ongoing motivation and direction. We call this 'practice leadership' to distinguish it from the broader sense of the management and leadership found in any organisation, to emphasise its focus on the quality of life of the individual served.

The chapter starts by examining some of the background literature on leadership in human services before reviewing research on the role of first-line managers in group homes for people with severe or profound intellectual disabilities, much of it carried out by our own colleagues at the Tizard Centre. Practice leadership is then defined and described, based on experience of training staff and working with organisations implementing active support. This is followed by a review of research on practice leadership – much of it recent or still under way – indicating how research in this area is developing. Finally, the chapter concludes by considering the importance of practice leadership and draws links to the wider organisational issues addressed in the following section.

Leadership in human services

Cherniss (1980, Chapter 6) explored the role that leadership and supervision played in reducing staff burnout in human services.

He noted that, consistent with other settings, supervisors in human services monitor and evaluate the work of their subordinates, to ensure sufficient accountability and conformity, to communicate important administrative decisions and to provide information for the organisation's leadership. However, he also drew attention to the way in which, unlike industrial or business settings, supervisors in the human services perform a professional development role as well as an administrative control role. He describes supervision in this context as a 'mentor relationship', through which staff will be supported to grow and develop and to manage the role they play. How good the supervision is, therefore, is likely to impact on staff's experience.

Thus, Cherniss suggested that there were several kinds of support staff seek from their supervisors:

- technical assistance (e.g. able to suggest better ways to handle difficult problems)

- support through the emotional demands of care work

- information, modelling and feedback, including corrective but constructive feedback

- support as buffer and advocate, protecting staff from external pressures and standing up for their interests.

Overall, staff need supervisors to be responsive as well as to give them autonomy. Cherniss suggests that a supervisor who always offers formulations and advice to his or her staff could stifle their desire to work through problems on their own. Staff may find it more helpful if their supervisor helps them by asking questions, paraphrasing and listening:

> Most supervisors give direct suggestions, advice and interpretations most of the time…they do not help workers to examine their own feelings or to think through cases on their own…the optimal style of supervision will vary with the worker and the situation… the key is responsiveness. (Cherniss 1980, p.118–19)

Thus, the model of leadership emerging from this analysis involves *skilled professional advice and assistance* as well as administrative control, and an *educational and developmental role* rather than simple direction.

These components are also brought to the fore in recent work examining the organisational factors that need to be in place to enhance personal outcomes for people using intellectual disability services (Schalock *et al.* 2008), which identifies five key leadership characteristics:

> (1) communicate a shared vision that answers the question, 'what do we want to create?'; (2) encourage and support the power of personal mastery so that people can grow and develop insight and skills (Senge, 2006); (3) stress a systems perspective that involves action feedback (Richardson, 1990); (4) promote a community life context for quality of life, emphasizing the bridging role of organizations (DeWaele *et al.*, 2005; Schalock, Gardner and Bradley, 2007; Walsh *et al.*, 2006); and (5) focus on measuring personal outcomes and ensuring the transfer of knowledge throughout an entire organization to examine and understand ways that the organization can achieve these desired outcomes (Orthner and Bownen, 2004; Orthner *et al.*, 2006). (Schalock *et al.*, 2008, p.280)

Although these are characteristics of leadership at any level in services, they apply just as much to the role of the team leader attempting to improve outcomes for the individuals his or her team supports. As well as emphasising the importance of skilled professional advice and assistance and an educational and developmental role, this approach also emphasises the role of the leader in *negotiating and influencing demands from the wider organisation*, a role already identified as problematic in earlier research (Thousand, Burchard and Hasazi 1986).

The role of first-line managers leading staff support teams

The largest body of work on the role of first-line managers in services for people with intellectual disabilities has been that carried out by researchers based at the University of Minnesota (Hewitt *et al.* 2004; Larson *et al.* 2007; Larson and Hewitt 2005). This work has identified a very large number of competencies (142 in the original work, in 14 domains) that first-line managers must have, including some they need to possess on appointment and some that are a priority for training. Clement and Bigby (2010, p.198), reviewing this material in a Victorian context, note that there will be some variation in the range of tasks required of managers, but the overwhelming impression is that of the breadth and complexity of the manager's job. How do people make sense of this difficult role?

In an exploratory study, Beadle-Brown, Vallis and Mansell (2006) identified the tasks undertaken by managers leading staff support teams, how important they thought these tasks were and how much time they took. They found that the role of manager was extremely varied, with many different tasks rated as important. Those rated as most important were those that involved directly working with service users and ensuring that the service met their physical and emotional needs, maintaining an effective work environment, ensuring service quality is maintained (usually with a focus on ensuring that regulatory standards were met) and helping staff to solve difficulties with users when they arise. Some managers also rated budget management and their own personal development as very important. However, ratings of importance for tasks such as managing the performance of individual staff, assisting staff to solve difficulties with users, providing supervision and appraisal, guiding and directing staff in the management of challenging behaviour, directing the work of the staff team and delivering training to staff were not rated amongst the most important. In terms of time spent in various tasks, Beadle-Brown *et al.* (2006) found that managers reported that they spent most time directly engaging with service users and ensuring all service administration was performed effectively. Practice leadership tasks did not feature in the most frequent tasks for managers.

This study was based on managers' self-reports and so might have been subject to social desirability bias in their responses. Gifford, Beadle-Brown and Mansell (2006) carried out a time-budget study which showed, conversely, that the activity most frequently engaged in was 'administration', with 'direct support work' featuring as the fourth most widely cited task. The findings additionally showed that 78 per cent of documented tasks did not directly involve service users and just 21 per cent of time was, on average, spent on tasks involving service users. It seems likely that managers are in fact responding to the high volumes of administrative responsibilities they are required to assume and a failure to manage their time effectively. In this study, 33 per cent of participants considered that administration detracted from other elements of their role, 41 per cent contended that the volume of administration they were required to complete was too great, and 60 per cent suggested that administrative demands had increased in recent years. 'Time management' was the lowest-ranking skill that participants considered an effective manager should possess, and a relatively high proportion – 30 per cent – reported either that they did not manage their time effectively or that they did not have any specific time-management strategies. One-third of the managers reported that, due to staff, personal or multiple disturbances, they had not achieved everything they had hoped to achieve during their documented shifts.

These data have to be interpreted with caution because even time-budget studies are based on self-reports. Generally, very little is still known about what first-line managers actually do, and there is variation in the research. For example, Clement and Bigby (2010, p.203) found that 12 managers reported spending 40 per cent of their time on activities relating to direct support to residents in the group homes they managed. Nevertheless, it seems clear that administrative demands and time management are important issues if the primary focus of team leadership is to be improving the practice of supporting the people the team serves.

Interviews with the managers participating in the study by Gifford et al. (2006) also identified a further difficulty. Ford and Honnor (2000) noted that managers of residential homes consistently identified the recruitment, training and retention of high-quality staff to be amongst the most challenging problems they face. Similarly, Gifford et al. (2006) found that managers discussed a range of problems relating to staff, with reports that staff lack initiative and aspiration, require too much support and could be difficult to work with. As one quotation illustrates: 'Every supervision, every staff meeting will be very similar to the last one... you're dealing with people with very limited focus and aspiration... You ask, "What do you do?" and they say, "I don't know, whatever you tell me"' (Gifford 2007, p.519).

Hewitt et al. (2004, p.132) describe the role of manager as 'impossible and chaotic', with the notion that the manager darts from one task to the next, with frequent interruptions and competing priorities and demands. Despite their apparent recognition of the importance of supporting the people their team serves, these managers seem to be beset with administrative responsibilities and face responsibility for supporting staff who they may not feel they have the skills to help effectively.

Practice leadership

Clement and Bigby (2010, p.202 *et seq.*) point out that 'practice leadership' is an emergent concept in need of further development. It needs to be not so closely tied to the idea of active support that it has nothing to say about the wider range of leadership tasks for the support team, but it also needs to be not drawn so widely that it simply encompasses everything managers are given to do. A further caution, relating to the research described above, is that research on group home managers may have some limits when considering the role of practice leadership in more individualised family-controlled services using direct payments or individual budgets. The intention of these models is to reduce bureaucracy and increase focus on the quality of life of the disabled person being supported (Leadbeater 2004); in so far as that is achieved, it may have implications for the skills required of first-line managers.

Mansell *et al.* (2005) defined practice leadership by managers as the development and maintenance of good staff support for the people served, through:

- focusing, in all aspects of their work as manager, on the quality of life of service users and how well staff support this

- allocating and organising staff to deliver support when and how service users need and want it

- coaching staff to deliver better support by spending time with them providing feedback and modelling good practice

- reviewing the quality of support provided by individual staff in regular one-to-one supervision and finding ways to help staff improve it

- reviewing how well the staff team is enabling people to engage in meaningful activity and relationships in regular team meetings and finding ways to improve it.

Thus, practice leadership is conceptualised here as more than just coaching or modelling, although these are clearly very important aspects of the role. Ashman *et al.* (2010) note that although practice leadership is primarily a role for those providing day-to-day supervision and leadership for staff, all levels of management within an organisation have a role to play in leading practice. These issues are addressed in the next chapter.

There are three core interrelated components of the role of practice leader as implied by the definition above. The first is that practice leaders need to focus in all aspects of their work on the quality of life of the people they support and how well staff support this. The second is that practice leaders need to allocate and organise staff to deliver support when and how service users need and want it. Finally, they have to help staff to improve the support they provide over time.

Focusing, in all aspects of their work as manager, on the quality of life of service users and how well staff support this

This component is concerned with recognising the true purpose of the support being provided to individuals with severe or profound intellectual disabilities, giving priority to it and defending it against other pressures and influences. It follows that the first requirement for a good practice leader is that he or she understands and is committed to the goal of improving quality of life of the person or people his or her team supports. This is the sense of passion and vocation Clement and Bigby (2010, p.200) identify as potentially key attitudinal orientations, and it reflects the importance, already described in Chapter 3, attached by people using services to selecting staff with the right attitudes.

Commitment to improving quality of life also needs to be matched by a good understanding and skill in providing active support to enable people to achieve it. Since this is a leadership position, the team leader already needs to be skilled and experienced at providing active support.

Given this commitment and skill, the core of this component of practice leadership is the practice leader's behaviour in consistently giving priority to good support, against the other conflicting pressures his or her team faces. He or she has to demonstrate through his or her actions and words that ensuring that the individuals he or she supports experience the best possible quality of life is the primary task of the team he or she leads and that this is more important than activities such as managing resources, meeting standards or completing paperwork. Of course, these types of activities may form part of the role of the person managing the service, but should not be seen as more important than the quality of life of the people the team serves.

Giving priority to the provision of good support draws particularly on the skills of the practice leader in negotiating and influencing demands from the wider organisation, and on his or her educational and developmental role with his or her own team. Explaining why some organisational or administrative demands have to be set aside for the moment; or how some administrative process gets in the way of a person's quality of life; or why the care inspector should focus on what the individual person being supported is enabled to actually do, rather than on how tidy his or her room is; all of these place a requirement on the practice leader to explain and persuade (and they also have implications for the organisation's support of the practice leader). In doing so, the practice leader is also modelling and demonstrating to his or her own team and others around him or her the reasons why good support is important and why it is worth arguing for.

Allocating and organising staff to deliver support when and how service users need and want it

Practice leaders need to support staff to work as a team, in such a way as to ensure they provide enabling support that is consistent, predictable for the individual and led by the individual's preferences and agendas. Chapter 4 outlined the main issues and some of the strategies that can be used to do this. It noted that the most important outcome of the use of tools and plans to organise staff support is the shared understanding that comes from the discussion of what works for each individual in order to develop the plans. Practice leaders need to be able to lead these discussions in team meetings, other planning meetings and during handover periods on shifts so that they ensure that all staff understand what is required of them and how they are to support the individuals with whom they work.

Practice leaders also lead the team to work out that what is important to, and important for, the person is recognised, understood and acted on by staff. For some people, support profiles regarding particular activities (e.g. those that involve something that is of higher risk for that individual), communication needs or behaviour support plans will also need to be developed. Although the person's key worker or an external professional may take the lead on developing some of these, the practice leader will need to ensure that all staff have read, understood and act on such plans and profiles. They may also need to input into assessment and planning processes run by other parts of the health and social care system to ensure that the plans reflect all the knowledge that the team holds about the individual.

Helping staff to shape up the quality of support

The third core component of practice leadership is the way the practice leader helps the team he or she leads to shape up the quality of support they provide. Mansell *et al.* (2005) identified three aspects of this task:

- identifying areas to improve

- coaching and modelling

- reviewing and confirming improvement.

IDENTIFYING AREAS TO IMPROVE

One of the roles of the practice leader in any setting is to identify the areas in which staff practice needs to improve. There are a number of ways in which this can be done. These are not mutually exclusive and indeed using a variety of techniques will be important.

First, practice leaders should encourage staff to reflect on their own practice and to identify areas that they would like to improve. As Cherniss (1980, pp.118–19) notes, team members may want to identify and raise issues themselves and work with the practice leader in thinking through possible solutions, rather than being told what changes are needed. Encouraging reflective practice can take place in individual supervision meetings or the practice leader might ask how staff thought an activity had gone and then give staff the opportunity to say what they might do differently next time and what they might need to help them do it differently. This can also be done, as a team, in meetings reviewing the quality of support provided.

Given the possible cultural difficulties of openly discussing the quality of work performance in many employment situations, practice leaders need to build a culture in which staff feel comfortable and confident to think about their own support, to recognise when things have gone well and they have provided good support, and when things have not worked for them or for the individual they were supporting. Disclosing and reflecting on the quality of support may require the practice leader to lead by example, using his or her own performance as the basis for discussion in order to reassure team members and build a supportive team culture.

However, as well as encouraging individuals and the team to reflect on their practice, practice leaders should themselves spend time watching how team members provide support and identifying problems and issues that need to be overcome. This requires, of course, that they are alongside members of their team while they are supporting people so that they can see what is happening. Although informal opportunities will be important, it is also likely that practice leaders will need to make sure that they are covering all their team members within a reasonable period. Commenting on the quality of support itself demonstrates its importance so that there is a symbolic value to this kind of observation as support is being provided.

COACHING AND MODELLING

Modelling is essentially 'demonstrating the desired behaviours and skills (in this case, providing good person-centred support) to staff so that they will be able to replicate them in their own work' (Ashman *et al.* 2010, p.119). Modelling person-centred active support is important because it reinforces the message of enabling people to be engaged in meaningful activities and relationships and thus helping them to experience social inclusion, real choice and growth in independence. It is also important because it demonstrates to staff that practice leaders can work in this way and that leaders are not asking staff to do anything that they could or would not do themselves, which is an important part of building a positive and supportive culture.

Clement and Bigby (2010, p.224) described two types of modelling: first, passive modelling in which practice leaders take everyday opportunities to demonstrate good practice so that staff will pick up on this and learn that this is what they should be aiming to do, primarily while they are working on shift alongside staff; and, second, active modelling, where practice leaders use incidental opportunities to demonstrate how staff should be working during a shift or a visit to the service (e.g. when new activities take place, problems occur or poor practice is seen).

In order to be able to model, those leading staff teams need to be working alongside staff, available to see what staff are doing and also confident in their own practices. Although modelling is an important aspect of shaping up staff practices, it is not the only tool for practice leaders to use. Coaching adds the elements of observation and feedback, goal setting and empowering and skilling staff in reflective practices to help staff improve the support they provide.

Ashman *et al.* note that:

> coaching has elements of several different approaches and can often be confused with these specific approaches. Coaching is not the same as modelling, training, demonstrating, supervision, instruction or mentoring, although it might include one or more of these elements…a process that happens in the work situation (not away from work like training or in supervision) between a coach and a person being coached… (2010, p.122)

They describe the steps involved in successful coaching as *Focus, Explain and demonstrate, Observe* and *Feedback*. Figure 5.1 is adapted from Figure 1 in Ashman *et al.* (2010, p.122). Thus, coaching is a more formal, directed and structured process than modelling.

1. Focus

- Establish rapport.
- Communicate your expectations.
- Find out what the staff member can do and find difficult through observation and discussion in supervision.

2. Explain and demonstrate

- Explain the steps of the task.
- Explain why they are important.
- Demonstrate them.

3. Observe

- Staff member explains and demonstrates what the coach demonstrated in step 2.

4. Feedback

- Coach staff member and discuss performance in step 3.

5. Repeat if necessary.

Figure 5.1 Steps to successful coaching

REVIEWING AND CONFIRMING IMPROVEMENT

Mansell *et al.* (2005) identify two core resources for practice leaders formally to review and confirm improvement in the quality of support provided – supervision and team meetings. In our experience, these are both under pressure from shortage of resources in many services, so that it is not uncommon to meet staff who have not had the opportunity to discuss their work either individually or collectively. It seems inconceivable that it would be possible to provide the kind of reflective, coordinated practice required without providing them.

Supervision is an opportunity for senior and more experienced staff members to discuss and review how well an individual member of the team is doing, to check the individual's self-evaluation with their own and for the individual team member to get guidance and help to improve what he or she does from a more experienced practitioner. It is an opportunity both to recognise and to reward good practice and to pick up any issues in a way that helps staff to be able to reflect and improve their practice in the future. Ashman *et al.* (2010, p.107) note that supervision is one of the most important tools available to practice leaders. They suggest that as part of supervision, practice leaders need to:

- ensure staff understand what is required and are committed to supporting people successfully

- develop the individual's skills and confidence in working with the people effectively

- provide effective leadership and motivate the staff member to continue to develop person-centred active support in all aspects of his or her work

- provide regular feedback on performance and the development of consistent approaches based on direct observation and SMART (i.e. specific, measurable, acceptable, realistic and timely) goal planning

- help the staff member to filter and prioritise competing needs and responsibilities to ensure person-centred support is the key task

- identify person development needs in relation to practice and person-centred active support.

While supervision focuses on the individual members of staff, team meetings give practice leaders the opportunity to review how well the team is enabling people to engage in meaningful activity and relationships and to review the balance of activities, consistency of approach and pursuit of goals of inclusion, independence and choice with the whole team. It gives the opportunity to solve problems and agree ways forward to support people better, thus improving consistency of approach.

Ashman *et al.* (2010, p.88) suggest that team meetings provide a forum to:

- promote the importance of engagement and person-centred approaches

- give clear information about practice

- share information and solve problems

- acknowledge and celebrate successes and good practice
- give feedback on performance
- review the extent of engagement in meaningful activities and relationships by the people they support
- review current practice and support arrangements
- develop consistent approaches to support
- identify opportunities to develop existing and introduce new activities and relationships.

They go on to remind the reader that:

> supporting people to actively participate in a wide range of activities and relationships is complex, so it is important that team members have a forum in which they can raise concerns for discussion if they think things are not working as well as they should. Team meetings provide regular opportunities to review progress for each of the people being supported, noting success, resolving problems and working out new arrangements. While it is not realistic to expect that staff and organisational issues will not be part of team meetings, care needs to be taken to prevent them from dominating. Dealing with issues about the people we support first, before dealing with organisational communication and staff issues, makes it more likely that proper attention is given to needs and preferences of those being served. (2010, p.88)

Supervision and team meetings are simply mechanisms to set the opportunity for review, learning and improvement. They can be used well or less well for this purpose, and some of the concerns expressed in Chapter 4 apply as much to meetings as to paperwork. Recently, Sanderson and Smull (2011) have promoted a set of tools for 'person-centred thinking'. These are intended not so much to specify the practical arrangements for review as to provide tools the support team can use to think through the issues they face. They are based on Essential Lifestyle Planning (Smull and Burke-Harrison 1992) but are relevant to support as well as planning. The seven tools are:

- 'Important to/Important for': A way to decide what matters to the individual being supported, and what matters for them whether they recognise it or not.

- 'The doughnut': Distinguishes core responsibilities of people providing support from areas where they can use judgement and creativity.

- Matching staff: A structure to look at what skills/supports and what 'people characteristics' make for good matches between people providing support and the person they are supporting.

- Communications: Key information about how a person communicates.

- 'What's working/not working': Analyses an issue from multiple perspectives.

- '4+1 questions': Focuses on learning from team efforts.

- 'Learning log': A structure that captures details of learning within specific activities and experiences.

The key lesson from this section is that ways have to be found to sustain a creative, reflective dialogue about the quality of support being provided to the individuals being served by the team. This dialogue requires opportunities to take place (such as team meetings and individual supervision), but it also requires processes that enable members of the team to share their experiences and learn from them. Taking the three leadership requirements identified at the beginning of this chapter – skilled professional advice and assistance, an educational and developmental role and negotiating and influencing demands from the wider organisation – we are struck by the level and breadth of skill required of these practitioners. Whether this is adequately reflected in arrangements for training and employment is beyond the scope of this book but is a topic worth some attention.

Research on practice leadership
Research on practice leadership is in its early stages, but in a number of studies we and colleagues have begun to explore the relationship between practice leadership, the quality of active support and

engagement in meaningful activity and relationships of people with severe or profound intellectual disabilities.

Beadle-Brown *et al.* (submitted; 2008) used a staff questionnaire to gain insight into staff's perceptions of whether their first-line manager engaged in the activities that would be classed as practice leadership. The questionnaire explored the frequency, usefulness and focus of team meetings and supervisions, and whether their manager observed and, if so, what he or she focused on, whether he or she modelled and whether he or she gave feedback that was useful. A 12-item practice leadership index was constructed from the responses to the questionnaire.

As the key hypothesis was that practice leadership is important to shaping up staff performance and thus the quality of active support, the focus of the Beadle-Brown *et al.* (submitted; 2008) papers was on whether there was a link between practice leadership and *change* in active support (which led to *change* in engagement in meaningful activity and relationships). In an initial study, they reported that engagement (using a rating scale rather than momentary time-sampling observation) had increased significantly over time and that active support and level of ability together explained over half of the variance in engagement at the second point in time in the study. Whether there had been any change in engagement over time was explained by whether there had been any change in active support (40% of the variance) and whether people were living in a supported living setting at second data collection (2% of the variance) – that is, those in supported living settings and those who were receiving better active support were more likely to experience increases in engagement.

Thus, change in active support appeared to be important in explaining change in engagement in meaningful activity and relationships. What explained change in active support? A series of stepwise regression analyses and moderation and mediation analyses were conducted for a sample of people who lived in services with fewer than 20 per cent of staff having been working in the service for over five years (it had been found that where there was a more established staff team, there had been less change in active support). Three variables were entered into the analysis: the practice leadership index, score on a measure of teamwork and an index that had been created to look at staff motivation – staff had been asked to rate the importance to them and to their manager of a range of tasks, some of which focused on client-centred activities and enabling activities and some on staff-centred and administration tasks.

The analysis found that only two things appeared to explain change in active support: staff motivation explained 3.4 per cent of the variance and experience of team working explained 18 per cent of the variance. Together, these explained approximately one-fifth of the variance in change in active support. Although practice leadership did not emerge as significant in the final model, univariate analysis of practice leadership on change in active support found that it explained 9 per cent of the variance in change in active support and as such interactions with the other variables may be taking place. However, further analysis to explore the relationship between these three variables found no significant moderation or mediation effects.

This analysis was a preliminary attempt to model the factors that impact on the implementation of active support over time. The indices used were derived post hoc, were not designed for the purpose and were limited in nature. The measure of change in engagement in this study was limited as the baseline data had been collected using a rating scale of estimates of engagement. In addition, not everyone had experienced an improvement in active support and the average practice leadership index was not very high (41%). Although half the staff reported that observations by managers focused on supporting engagement, less than a fifth said this happened at least monthly, included useful feedback or involved modelling of how to provide better support.

When collecting the observational data reported for Study 2 in Beadle-Brown *et al.* (2011) submitted, the practice leadership index was used in conjunction with revised indices of task importance (as an indication of motivation) and a new knowledge index. Practice leadership scores were slightly higher on average than they had been in the Study 1 – 52 per cent compared to 41 per cent. Practice leadership scores were also slightly higher in teams providing good active support (mean 54%, n=118) compared to weak or mixed active support (mean 49%, n=72; z=2.223 p<0.05). At individual staff level in Study 2, managers were rated as much more likely to observe staff at least monthly, to model good support and to give useful feedback both in general and in supervision.

There was a significant correlation between the practice leadership index and change in active support over time for those for whom data had been available from an earlier evaluation (0.437, p<0.001). Regression analysis of a selection of staff team-related variables on active support scores found that the final model explained 35 per cent of the variance but only adaptive behaviour of the people supported emerged as significant. However, when the regression analysis was repeated for change in active support scores over time, only two variables were entered into the final model – quality of management and practice leadership – which explained 32 per cent of the variance. Only quality of management emerged as significant (see Table 5.1). Analysis looking at the impact of each of practice leadership and quality of management on change in active support revealed that they both explained 13 per cent of the variance. Further analysis using mediation and moderation analysis found that there was no interaction between the two but that there was full mediation, with quality of management mediating the effect of practice leadership on change in active support. When management quality was below the median there was no significant difference in active support irrespective of whether staff reported high or low practice leadership. Only when quality of management was higher (above the median), did better practice leadership produce a significant difference. Thus practice leadership appears only to be important in the presence of good quality management.

Table 5.1 Summary of the regression analysis on active support and change in active support over time for study 2 from Beadle-Brown *et al.* (submitted).

Active support at T2					
Main effect	F=38.763, p<0.001, df 1,72, R2 = 0.350, R2 adj = 0.341				
Variables	B	St error	Beta	T	R2/R2 change
Adaptive behaviour	0.225	0.036	0.592	6.226***	0.35
Task important for staff					excluded
Role conflict					excluded
Manager had practice leadership training					excluded
Change in active support					
Main effect	F=32.887 p<0.001; df 1,71; R2 =0.317, R2 adj 0.307				
Variables	B	St error	Beta	T	R2/R2 change
Quality of management	1.535	0.268	0.563	5.735***	0.317
Practice leadership			0.097	0.852	excluded

Although the sample was not big enough to carry out regression analysis, Beadle-Brown *et al.* (2012) found that staff teams rated practice leadership more strongly after the implementation of active support than before, even though ratings had been quite high to start with. Practice leadership scores at staff level increased from 74 per cent (37–94) to 83 per cent (65–95). It was not possible to conduct statistical analysis on this data as staff questionnaires could not be matched across baseline and follow-up. However, using an analysis of the data at user level where the mean team level score on the practice leadership index was used, it was found that, at follow-up, participants were supported by teams that were experiencing significantly higher levels of practice leadership as rated by staff themselves.

One of the limitations of the research to date is that it has relied on staff perceptions of whether their managers were providing practice leadership. Of course, this is an important view to take – if staff do not think they are receiving practice leadership, then, even if their manager thinks he or she is providing practice leadership, it may not be effective. Current work in Australia with Bigby and colleagues is focused on developing and testing an observational measure of practice leadership, in addition to asking managers and staff to rate practice leadership. This measure combines observations, interviews with managers and, where possible, staff and a review of plans and paperwork used in the service.

Despite the limited amount of research and its exploratory nature, it does seem clear that practice leadership is a central issue in enabling people providing support to do a good job for people with severe or profound intellectual disabilities. The implication of this is that attention needs to be given to the training, career development and support of practice leaders, and also to how their time is to be protected for the important work they do from the many other responsibilities with which first-line managers have become encumbered.

Conclusion

The fact that, in practice, most people supporting individuals with severe or profound intellectual disabilities will work in teams means that these teams need organising. As explained in the last chapter, this cannot be left to chance because of the evidence that teams develop norms and approaches that are self-serving or antithetical to the goal of improving quality of life for the people they serve. That places a special emphasis on the first-line managers leading these teams. They are the custodians of the vision of the team and its culture.

This role is not characterised by administrative control, in which the supervisor acts as a conduit for organisational policies and procedures to team members who are just expected to do what they are told. Nor is it simply being one of the team – working alongside other members in some kind of quasi-democratic equality. Instead, it is a distinctive leadership role in which the person has sufficient sapiential authority to guide his or her team, the skills of a teacher and mentor in order to develop them and the ability to defend good practice against other pressures.

These pressures often come from the wider organisation of which the team is part. This is the subject of the next chapter.

CHAPTER 6

The Organisational Context

The contribution of the leader of the team providing support appears to be an important factor, perhaps the most important factor, ensuring the success of active support. As argued in the previous chapter, leadership in practice – the coaching and mentoring of the support team to provide help in the way that best enables engagement in meaningful activity and relationships by the people they support – and leadership in terms of sustaining the team's focus and commitment appear to be critical to the success of active support.

Good practice leadership is not, however, the only relevant factor. The wider organisational context is important in how it supports or hinders active support. For example, it might be thought that organisations espousing the values of community living and social inclusion, or those that have more highly trained staff or where staff turnover is lower, would be better at providing active support. Certainly the organisational context seems to be important. Although early demonstration projects (Felce, de Kock and Repp 1986; Jones *et al.* 1999, 2001a; Mansell and Beasley 1993) showed very dramatic results in organisations that might be thought to be quite ordinary, the point is that the context for these projects included the involvement of the researchers. That in itself made the organisations special (not everyone welcomes the involvement of researchers) and the researchers themselves were able to impose special conditions and provide extra motivation and skill that the organisation itself might not have possessed. One of the reasons for the relatively slow and partial take-up of active support might be that these factors were weak or missing in the organisations involved.

This chapter explores the organisational context for implementing active support, drawing both on the (rather limited amount of) research and also on our own experience of working with many different organisations trying to put active support into practice. The first part of the chapter briefly reviews research on the effect of organisational factors in residential settings for people with intellectual disabilities, drawing out some of the implications of the research. This is followed by an analysis of the organisational context, distinguishing the development of skills through training of different kinds from the creation of a motivational framework in which skills will be used. The way these issues have been addressed in some of the organisations with which we have worked is described next. Finally, we turn to the question of monitoring progress in implementing and sustaining active support, looking at the approaches that senior managers can use to evaluate progress.

Background

Assumptions about what factors might influence staff care practices in residential services for people with intellectual disabilities underpin most service management and much of the movement to reform services for people with intellectual disabilities over the last 40 years. Factors that have been studied, in their own right or in relation to care practices, include:

1. Setting characteristics: the type of service (Emerson and Hatton 1994; Tizard 1960) and size (Balla 1976; Landesman-Dwyer *et al.* 1980; Stancliffe 1997; Tossebro 1995).

2. Staffing: the ratio of staff to residents (Felce *et al.* 1991; Harris *et al.* 1974; Mansell *et al.* 1982b); staff qualifications and experience (Allen, Pahl and Quine 1990); receipt of training and staff knowledge (Bradshaw *et al.* 2004; Cullen 1988; Hastings, Reed and Watts 1997; Jones *et al.* 1999; Levy, Levy and Samowitz 1994; Mansell *et al.* 2003); turnover (Baumeister and Zaharia 1987; Felce, Lowe and Beswick 1993; Hatton and Emerson 1998; Lakin *et al.* 1982); attitudes (Department of Health and Social Security 1979; Henry *et al.* 1996; Kordoutis *et al.* 1995; Stenfert Kroese and Fleming 1992).

3. Organisational hygiene: job satisfaction (Dyer and Quine 1998; Hatton *et al.* 1999); stress (Elliott and Rose 1997; Hatton *et al.*

1995a; Potts *et al.* 1995; Rose 1995, 1997); role clarity and conflict (Allen *et al.* 1990).

4.   Management: autonomy of managers (King *et al.* 1971); systems for organising care (Emerson *et al.* 2000a; Felce *et al.* 2002b; Jacobson 1990; Reid and Whitman 1983).

None of these factors has been simply and consistently identified as predicting good care practices. As Hastings, Remington and Hatton (1995) noted, it is likely that factors influencing care practices operate in combination. For example, Jones *et al.* (2001b) showed that both classroom training and practical training were required for staff to change their practice in using active support. There is also some evidence that effects may be contingent on particular situational factors. Early studies of the effect of size on care practices (Balla 1976; King *et al.* 1971) suggested little or no relationship. These were studies of relatively large settings. Only when very small-scale community-based services were studied did size become important (Tossebro 1995).

This implies that attention should be given to factors that might be specific to particular service models – different factors may be important in different kinds of service setting. It also implies that it is important to study a wider range of service and staff characteristics than has typically been studied in the past and to combine multivariate with comparative methods to determine the relative importance of particular variables. Recent studies which focused on group homes for people with severe or profound intellectual disabilities have found very limited evidence for the effect of service and staff characteristics on care practices and outcome. Felce *et al.* (2002a, 2002b) studied 29 staffed houses, looking at staff numbers, qualifications, experience, systems for organising care and management milieu. They found evidence that higher staff ratio and more experienced staff predicted high levels of assistance from staff, but that systems for organising care and milieu did not. In a larger study of 60 houses, Felce *et al.* (2003) also found evidence for the effect of staff ratio and also evidence that systems for organising care were important in influencing the amount of staff attention received by residents. Mansell *et al.* (2003) studied 76 staffed houses, looking at staff numbers, experience, turnover, seniority and participation in in-service training. They found that no organisational or staffing characteristics predicted extent of active support.

In a study of a wider range of factors, including staff attitudes, teamwork, leadership, role clarity, satisfaction and stress, Mansell *et al.* (2008) found a complex picture in which specific items on measures used were often significant, rather than whole scale scores. They found that a group of services providing active support had more staff with a professional qualification, staff who were more likely to think that challenging behaviour was caused by lack of stimulation, had attitudes more in line with a policy of community care, rated most care tasks as less difficult and were more organised to deliver active support. A comparison group of staff were more likely to think that challenging behaviour was learned negative behaviour, but experienced more teamwork and were more satisfied with their jobs. Multivariate analysis identified a range of staff and organisational variables associated with engagement and active support. Professional qualification, knowledge and experience appeared to be important, as did some staff attitudes, clear management guidance, more frequent supervision and team meetings, training and support for staff to help residents engage in meaningful activity.

Overall, then, there is no clear understanding of the role of organisational factors in promoting active support. The implication is that those people leading organisations implementing active support have to draw on the distilled experience of the management textbook and on trying to learn useful lessons from those organisations that have been more successful in sustaining good practice, as much as on any particular research study. The other relevant observation is that there is a large number of potential factors that could plausibly influence implementation. Success may therefore require organisations to attend to many different things at the same time. Attending only to one or two (e.g., just training staff) is unlikely to be enough.

Supporting good staff performance

Mansell *et al.* (2005) offer the maxim that 'the fundamental fact' for managers is that staff performance is the product of *skill* and *motivation*. If staff are to provide person-centred active support, they must have the skills to do so and they must want to do so. Having the skills means possessing the relevant knowledge, but it also means being practised enough to use that knowledge in the hands-on situation of providing support. Wanting to do so includes both the person's own values and attitudes but also the effect of factors in the organisation that help or hinder providing active support. Thus, all the many factors identified in the research described above – the qualifications and training of staff, the policies and procedures of the organisation, its recruitment and personnel practices, and so on – act through their effect on the skill and motivation of the people providing direct support.

Skills and motivation are both important, and they are mutually reinforcing. If staff cannot see any point in the people they serve engaging in meaningful activity and relationships, then they will not want to take part in training. Even if these members of staff are successfully trained, they won't put the training into practice or will give up as soon as they face difficulties. If they are committed but the organisation puts practical obstacles in their way or signals to them that active support is not really important, then their commitment is likely to wane. Similarly, if staff are keen to implement person-centred active support but do not get the help they need to become skilled at providing it, then they will find it hard to maintain their commitment.

Training

All of the active support training materials emphasise that training requires both a classroom and a practical component. The classroom component in our most recent version of the training materials (Mansell *et al.* 2005) is focused on three main goals:

- The first of these is understanding the rationales for active support. This relates to the discussion in Chapter 4 about the development of group norms that favour active support and enabling people to engage in meaningful activity and relationships. It has become increasingly clear to us that it is important for people providing support to be able to explain what they are doing and why. Being able to recount to themselves the reasons for a particular course of action is likely to help people prepare to do it and do it well. The ability to explain what needs to be done and why is important in discussing with colleagues in the support team what should be done; it is also important preparation for and in discussion with other audiences – families, neighbours, shopkeepers, managers, inspectors and so on – who judge the work of the team. These are all approaches used in cognitive behavioural therapy to help people develop and keep to desired repertoires (Meichenbaum 1977). This cannot be taken for granted: in a study by Totsika *et al.* (2008) which involved interviewing 37 staff about their experience of training in active support, staff working in the same team agreed about which elements of active support they were using in only 10 per cent of possible instances. Such a low level of knowledge implies a need for consciousness raising among staff if good teamwork is to be developed and defended.

- The second goal of classroom training in active support is that people should learn the principles or rules that should guide their action, rather than simply learning a set of activities to be carried out. Good active support involves enabling the people providing support to use their imagination and creativity to help the individual engage in meaningful activity and relationships, rather than constraining them to follow a precisely defined recipe. So the training does not teach people always to follow a hierarchy of assistance (ask–tell–show–guide) in providing help to enable the individual to succeed: instead, it teaches them a principle (graded assistance to ensure success) and encourages them to work out for themselves the best kind of help to provide. This approach is consistent with the 'try another way' model used in supported employment for people with severe or profound intellectual disabilities (Gold 1980a, 1980b) and with fostering generalisation of the skills learned by staff (Stokes and Baer 1977).

- Finally, classroom training in active support is intended to sensitise participants to the range of implementation issues. Thus, it addresses issues dealt with later in this chapter about overcoming obstacles to successful implementation (such as personnel policies or health and safety requirements). Even if people coming to be trained in active support are keen and enthusiastic, they will always identify factors in their current working arrangements that would hinder their provision of active support. It is important to acknowledge these and at least suggest a possible response to them. This might not always involve agreeing with the definition of the problem. Perhaps the most common objection is for people to say that they do not have enough staff to enable people to engage in meaningful activity and relationships; in modern community services, in our experience, this is very rarely true. The research suggests a very tenuous relationship between staff ratio and quality of support (Felce *et al.* 2003; Felce *et al.* 1991; Harris *et al.* 1974; Mansell *et al.* 1982b); the issue is more often a question of what is given priority by the staff team and their managers.

Classroom training is not likely to be sufficient to change actual practice on the job; for this, practical, 'hands-on', experiential training is needed (Anderson 1987; van Oorsouw *et al.* 2009). The goal is to help people move from verbal competence (in which they can describe what they should be doing and why) to practice competence (in which they actually do what is needed) (LaVigna 1994). Usually, this is carried out in the setting where support is being provided, with the whole team taking part and providing support to the individuals they serve. This kind of 'whole-environment training' (Hughes and Mansell 1990; Mansell *et al.* 1994; Whiffen 1984) addresses the opportunities and constraints actually faced by staff as they provide support and so provides practical solutions to many issues. It also demonstrates – to the people being supported, to staff themselves, to their managers and anyone else interested – that it is possible to enable people to engage in meaningful activity and relationships in spite of problems in practice. The form of hands-on training itself demonstrates the model of practice leadership described in the previous chapter. Typically, the trainer spends time with the members of the support team, coaching them in providing active support to the individual(s) with whom they are working – watching them, giving constructive feedback, demonstrating alternatives and providing encouragement and advice. The trainer can also provide a useful challenge if people are denied access to activities they want to do because the proper equipment is not available or there are rules that get in the way of participation. In these situations a fresh pair of eyes may help find solutions.

Even where training cannot be carried out in the real situation, it is possible to deal with many of these issues. One model we have used when training trainers or practice leaders is to bring trainees together in a day centre, college, church hall or other venue with a kitchen and several other rooms, along with some assistant trainers with intellectual disabilities. For example, when training 40 team leaders from all over England, where visiting the home of each person supported by people on the course was impractical, the solution was to arrange with a day centre to have the 40 participants visit the centre (in two groups of 20). The trainees practised providing active support to people attending the day centre, who generally found the experience at least as interesting as the routine activities the centre provided. Trainees also practised observing and giving feedback to each other. Feedback from those trained in this way has generally been very positive.

It should be evident from the description given above that this is not a training package that can be picked up by any trainer and delivered to good effect. Whether in the classroom or hands-on, the training needs to be delivered by people with experience of actually providing active support. In many respects, the skills of the good active support trainer are those of the practice leader.

Some insight into the importance of the content and method of active support training comes from a small number of studies. Jones *et al.* (2001b) introduced active support in 74 group homes: in 22 houses, training was led by one of the researchers, with identified managers assisting; in 16, it was led by a manager who had participated in the first group, assisted by the researcher; and in 36 houses, it was undertaken independently by managers who had participated in the other two groups. Significant increases in assistance and resident engagement in activity were found in the first two groups, but not in the third, where the managers had failed to provide the hands-on training. The lack of change in the third group showed that the practical training was a necessary component. In a small pre-post study of five staff, Toogood (2008) found increases in assistance and engagement when only hands-on training was provided. However, a larger study by Totsika *et al.* (2010) showed no changes among 58 staff. In this study, 21 staff had received classroom-based training 13 months earlier, but this did not influence the result. There was some evidence of a short-term effect for people with aggressive behaviour. More recently, Riches *et al.* (2011) trained a specialist group of trainers to deliver classroom and hands-on training to 65 staff in teams supporting 22 people living in six houses. Although the study does not include any observational measures of staff performance or service-user outcomes, questionnaires from staff suggest that the training was enjoyable, relevant and helpful and that they learned new approaches, understood the feedback provided to them and thought the training would be of lasting benefit. There was no difference between responses relating to training provided by the trained trainers compared with the consultants.

The implication of these studies is that both classroom and hands-on training seem to be important; this is consistent with other research on training in intellectual disability services (van Oorsouw *et al.* 2009). Given the number of evaluation studies where largely non-professional staff have been trained over a relatively short period of a few days and have demonstrated clear improvements in the extent to which they offer active support, coupled with dramatic increases in engagement in meaningful activity, one should not be pessimistic about the feasibility of training, so long as the trainers are themselves skilled practitioners.

Motivation

Whether people use the skills they have depends on a range of factors that act as incentives or disincentives; we group these together under the general heading of motivation.

Although in much of the discussion below we refer to incentives and disincentives at work in the organisation, it is important to recognise that individual staff bring their own values and attitudes which affect the way they provide support to the people they serve (Emerson, Hastings and McGill 1994). In Chapter 3, we identified personal attitudes as an important underpinning of 'the enabling relationship'. These may be attitudes and beliefs about intellectual disability or about people with intellectual disabilities – about their intrinsic worth as people or how they should be treated – as documented by Wolfensberger (1975). They may, however, not be about intellectual disability but still have an important effect on the way people provide support to the individual with intellectual disabilities. For example, if staff come from a cultural background in which cleanliness and order is highly valued, they may find it more difficult to adapt to 'lower' standards of people they support, even if this means greater engagement in meaningful activity for these people. If they come from a cultural background in which banter and teasing are an important part of the staff subculture, they may find it difficult not to adopt these practices even when they provoke 'challenging' responses from the people they serve.

For some people, these values or beliefs or attitudes can be readily changed. For example, most organisations providing support to disabled people successfully teach their staff that, even if they come from a culture in which hitting children is commonplace, they should not hit the people they are supporting, even when their behaviour appears to be the same. The problem arises where personal behaviour is too deeply rooted to change. The implication is that people with personal values that are inimical to actively supporting greater independence, inclusion and control need to be identified and either not employed or their employment terminated.

Even if people start with supportive, or at least tolerant, values in relation to active support, their experience of work can lead to them becoming indifferent, demoralised or 'burned-out' (Cherniss 1980). Essentially, what happens, in the model described by Cherniss, is that people experience *stress* in their work as its demands exceed their ability to meet them; this stress leads to psychological *strain*, in the form of increased anxiety, tension, fatigue and exhaustion; and in order to contain this strain, the person develops strategies of *defensive coping*, such as withdrawal, detachment, cynicism and rigidity. There are similarities between this and institutionalism (Wing and Brown 1970) or institutional neurosis (Barton 1959), so that it may not be entirely inaccurate to say that staff, like the residents of institutions, become 'institutionalised'. There are also similarities with Goffman's (1968) explanation of inhuman treatment in institutions, in which the requirement to reconcile the demands of treating people well and the practical exigencies of institution life led staff to deal with these pressures in two ways. First, rather than attempt to rationalise the inconsistencies of role expected, some staff became dissatisfied and escaped to other work or through role distancing. Second, staff adopted an institutional ideology in which inconsistencies were redefined within the manifest aims of the institution; all activities were described as therapeutic. Complaints or protests were dealt with by treating them as part of the pathological behaviour of the patient, subject to treatment or to reinterpretation in terms acceptable to staff.

Thus, for the staff in the institution, behaviour that in normal society would be reprehensible came to be seen as acceptable. The relationship with the patient was instrumental, rather than personal, and practices could be administered to the patient as object, which could not be contemplated outside of this relationship.

What these different perspectives have in common is that, put into a position that they cannot make sense of, staff working in services supporting dependent people will reconcile the situation either by leaving or by redefining the practices they are forced by circumstance to do as reasonable and acceptable.

What kind of demands might lead to these problems? In our experience, there are two broad groups of issues that impose these kinds of demands on people supporting individuals with severe or profound intellectual disabilities, which can be summarised as *lack of resources* and *competing priorities*.

Lack of resources is not, primarily, about the number of people employed to provide support. Most people we have worked with have enough staff to provide substantially improved quality of life if they are properly organised, trained and led. Sometimes there are problems where vacancies in the team are left unfilled for so long that the support team develops a way of working with fewer members that does not support a good quality of life. Having done so, their perception of the situation may then lead them not to make the best use of extra staff when they are available (cf. Felce *et al.* 1991). The most common problem of lack of resources is lack of training, or, even more so, lack of skilled practice leadership. Providing good active support to people with severe or profound intellectual disabilities will often be difficult and challenging. For example, Bromley and Emerson (1995) found that staff supporting people with challenging behaviour reported that repetitiveness, hopelessness and lack of understanding of the person's behaviour were major sources of stress. Mansell and Elliott (2001) reported that 10 per cent of staff in their study reported negative consequences (typically distress or challenging behaviour) from the people supported when staff tried to involve them in activity. If the team providing support cannot get training (including hands-on training), or if the training they have received is not followed up with good practice leadership, then the difficulties they will face in trying to support individuals with more complex needs are likely to wear away at their ability to sustain their practice.

Competing priorities can also sap staff motivation if they cannot be resolved. However, in our experience, it is not so much the existence of competing priorities that is the problem, since the support team can often find creative ways of engaging with problems to resolve apparent conflicts. Much more important is the relative importance attached to quality of life and active support as opposed to other things. If, by its words and deeds, the organisation signals that active support is unimportant or optional, then staff are likely to respond to this by giving priority to what managers really want. The next chapter discusses this in relation to different 'person-centred approaches', which can be seen as alternative rather than complementary aspects of unified practice. However, sometimes the signals are not to do with support at all, but to do with administrative or management procedures. Examples we have found include:

- chief executives of non-profit organisations that provide support explaining that since they know nothing about active support they delegate all aspects of dealing with it to an assistant (inadvertently risking the message that it is not important enough for them to deal with)

- recruitment materials and processes that do not mention practice leadership, active support or quality of life, and that make no attempt to match people to the individuals they will be supporting

- promotion criteria focused on administrative or general management qualities, ignoring practice leadership

- publicity material, mission statements, annual reports, plans and policies that do not refer to engagement in meaningful activity and relationships as an important goal or to active support as a primary working method

- health and safety requirements that prevent people participating in the activities they want in order to protect the organisation from the perceived risk of litigation; for example, rules that no one other than staff may be in the kitchen when the cooker is on

- 'management training' that makes no mention of practice leadership, active support or quality of life

- more effective management of performance relating to administration than to active support.

It has seemed to us, faced with these mixed messages, that an obvious approach is to remove any confusion by aligning messages. We have therefore encouraged organisations with whom we have worked to review systematically every aspect of their work to see whether it helps provide active support.

Implementing active support

Figure 6.1 shows the series of steps taken by one English organisation, the Avenues Trust, which set out to implement active support in its services. Similar approaches have been used in other organisations with which we have worked and elsewhere (McVilly *et al.* 2011).

- Senior management day to develop strategy for implementation.
- Effort to align different elements of organisation (HR, training, quality assurance).
- Implementation and targets written into five-year business plan – at least 10 per cent increase in engagement in every service trained.
- Appointed person-centred active support coordinator.
- Collected baseline data in each of the six pilot services.
- Trained Quality Assurance staff to do detailed observations – pre-training and one year post-training.
- Launched PCAS with roadshows in each area.
- Trained service and senior managers as observers and introduced 'formal observation' using simple rating scale every six months.
- Trained service managers and senior managers as trainers and PCAS coordinator supported them to deliver training.
- Trained house managers as practice leaders.
- Trained staff – classroom based and hands-on (six pilot services, then nine, then 15 each year until all 60 had been trained).
- Reduced daily recording – team involvement in designing forms.
- Changed shift plans to put people supported at the centre of staff activity.
- Article on active support in every annual report and on staff forums, etc.

Figure 6.1 Summary of the steps involved in the implementation of person-centred active support in the Avenues Trust

At the senior level, managers and the trustees of the organisation got to know enough about active support that they could demonstrate a credible interest in its implementation, both through management processes and in their interactions with the people the organisation supports, their families and the staff who support them. The entire management team devoted a day to planning the implementation of active support, which was introduced through a series of 'roadshows'. The organisation's business plan was amended to include a goal of increasing engagement in meaningful activity and relationships by 10 per cent in every service. This clear leadership has also been a characteristic of other organisations with which we have worked, such as United Response and Golden City Support Services, who have had more success in implementing active support.

Following the model successfully developed earlier by United Response (Ashman and Beadle-Brown 2006) and used also by Golden City Support Services, the organisation created a post, reporting to senior managers, responsible for leading the training and also the evaluation of active support. Training encompassed not only classroom and hands-on training for front-line staff but additional training for practice leaders and for managers who were involved in delivering training. In United Response, a 'practice development team' of three people leads on this, and in Golden City Support Services, there is a practice leadership team of three people. In each case, these people are tasked with supporting managers in implementing active support, not with replacing or supplanting them. Their responsibility for observing practice gives them direct knowledge of what is really happening at the front line, and their line management at a senior level in the organisation makes this feedback available to senior managers. Thus they can provide skilled help to middle and first-line managers responsible for implementing active support, while having access to senior people to solve problems that cannot be dealt with locally, and they provide knowledge of how well active support is being implemented independently of routine reporting arrangements.

At the same time as training staff, an audit of the paperwork expected of front-line staff was undertaken to reduce the amount of time required, and other processes were amended so that they aligned with active support. For example, quality assurance processes were changed to involve regular observation of the amount and quality of staff support and of engagement in meaningful activity and relationships, rather than focus exclusively on checklists of standards. In Golden City Support Services, the 'back office' team have met regularly to review how their work has an impact on delivery of active support and to shape administrative practices to support it. This has meant that when changes have been proposed by regulators in, for example, accounting procedures, the finance staff of Golden City have been able to argue the case for arrangements that support rather than hinder good practice. This means that problems are identified early (because it is not necessary to wait until support staff identify them), by people seen as credible within the regulatory regime, who have a greater likelihood of influencing new requirements in the required direction.

A common problem is that first-line managers perceive a range of areas of good practice in which they are supposed to be taking the lead, but see these as alternatives rather than complementary approaches. So, for example, people say that they are not making progress in active support because they are focusing on person-centred planning, or total communication approaches, or other good things. We examine this in more detail in the next chapter, but an important approach developed by United Response has been to codify all these things into 'The Way We Work' (Ashman *et al.* 2010) so that there is a single coherent account into which all support fits and which makes plain that a comprehensive approach to providing support is required. This is what Clement and Bigby (2011) call a 'programme theory' for the service.

In Avenues Trust, the chief executive and the director of operations were visible in the organisation, following up news of good work by telephoning or visiting support teams to congratulate them. Every newsletter and annual report included articles describing good practice in active support. Similarly, in Golden City and in United Response, senior managers notice, respond to and can credibly examine the quality of active support.

Most of the steps described above focus primarily on processes within the organisation. Of course, organisations deliver support to disabled people in a wider environment in which funding and regulation also influence what they do. Thus, front-line staff are not only influenced by what they perceive to be the true priorities of their own managers but by what people from other organisations say about them and their work. Often, these external influences are not helpful. For example, in a study comparing the results of using established observational and rating scale measures of quality of life with the care standards ratings made by government inspectors in England, Beadle-Brown, Hutchinson and Mansell (2005) found no relationship between them at all. A follow-up study (Netten *et al.* 2010) of revised quality ratings also found little evidence that inspectors' judgements reflected objective indicators of quality of life. In our experience, care quality inspectors often tell mediocre services (mediocre in that they provide poor support to people with severe or profound intellectual disabilities) that they are doing well on the basis of their paperwork and the physical environment. This undermines management leadership and hinders improving the quality of life of the people served. Educating inspectors, or those such as lay visitors who perform a monitoring role, to defend good practice is therefore likely to be an important function of senior management.

An emerging example of this is evident in the work of Golden City Support Services, where occupational health and safety inspectors initially proposed restrictive interventions (higher fences, more locks, barriers and barricades) to reduce injuries to staff supporting individuals with serious challenging behaviour. Through an extensive process of discussion and negotiation (taking several years), inspectors have come to see that the most effective interventions, which respect the human rights and support the quality of life of individuals whose behaviour is challenging, are those labelled as 'positive behaviour support', within which active support is an important component. This required Golden City to translate the language they used into that of the health and safety system, progressively working through issues behind the scenes until a better understanding of what was best was agreed. Health and safety legislation in Victoria requires that employers adopt agreed 'safe methods of working' to mitigate risks in the workplace. There is, therefore, the prospect that inspectors will see active support and positive behaviour support as *required* working methods.

What these examples show is that a successful approach to implementation is *comprehensive*, in that it addresses many aspects of the way the organisation works, and it is *coordinated*, in that it attempts to align incentives for implementation. It is also *continuous*, in that the work to defend good practice continues as the organisation faces the ongoing issues of maintaining practice in the face of staff turnover and new pressures from inside and outside its boundaries.

Stages of implementation

Ian McLean, the Chief Executive of Golden City Support Services, identifies a series of stages that organisations implementing active support might go through (see Table 6.2). The point about this analysis is that he suggests that the primary focus of the managers leading the organisation needs to be different at different stages, so it is important for managers (and the rest of the organisation) to understand where they are in the implementation process in order to focus on the right priorities.

Table 6.1 Stages of implementing active support

Stage of implementation	Primary focus of management action
From interest to enthusiasm	Consciousness raising, seeking champions, gaining and giving permissions and mandates for change
From enthusiasm to commitment	Helping early adopters, setting up experiments and demonstration projects
From commitment to competence	Sorting out training programmes, leadership and management, back-room issues; spreading the number of good teams and team leaders
From competence to excellence	Focusing on non-performance, defining it as unacceptable and requiring good active support as a non-negotiable part of the job

In the first stage, when the organisation is moving from initial interest towards enthusiasm for the idea of using active support to improve the quality of life of the people it serves, the primary focus of management needs to be in raising consciousness about quality of life, how engagement in meaningful activity and relationships fits into the quality of life framework and how active support can make dramatic improvements in people's lives. This should start with the organisation's own staff (who will often be the main messenger to others and so must get the story straight from the outset), but, of course, it will also need to involve the people being supported, their families and advocates from the beginning. The medium of communication may include written material, but much more powerful evidence, for families and advocates in particular, is likely to come from seeing examples of good practice (by visiting or on film), hearing from people involved in exemplary projects and being able to meet and talk to the people involved.

This is also the stage when management need to seek out, among the people they support, their advocates, families and support teams, those who will be early champions for the new approach and who can be prepared to provide demonstration sites and experiments. A second important function for this group is that they will be ambassadors for the new ideas, both with external audiences (inspectors, funders) and also internally among other staff and families. Managers leading the organisation will need to give a strong message that they support the new direction and the activities of these champions, so that everyone is clear that they have a strong mandate. They may also need to explain and defend what they are doing to external audiences (regulators, funders, government, the rest of the sector).

In the first stage, the primary focus is on motivation – building commitment, vision and enthusiasm – rather than on skill development. As the organisation moves from enthusiasm to commitment, the management focus extends to helping early adopters, setting up experiments and demonstration projects. This often entails creating special rules that allow the innovators to depart from the way things are usually done so that they can establish good ways of working in the new model. Senior management become their champions, so that when families and support teams come up against obstacles, they can go to them to get the obstacle removed.

At this stage, most of the organisation is working as it did before, but everyone knows that there are new ideas being tried out. Senior management has created a space in which the innovation can be developed and strengthened. Moving from commitment to competence involves taking the learning from the innovation and using it to reshape the way the rest of the organisation works – sorting out training programmes, leadership and management, back-room issues such as finance and personnel arrangements – in order to spread the number of good teams and team leaders. This is the major period in which teams of people providing support to the people they serve change what they are doing, and this ripples back through the organisation so that administrative procedures are adjusted to help sustain this process. Senior management attention is focused on the people trying to do well, helping them solve problems that come up as they do so.

The last stage in this sequence is moving from competence to excellence. Here senior management attention shifts away from the people now providing relatively consistent, good active support towards those who are continuing to fail to do so. These services are important not only because they are providing less good quality of life to the people they support but also because their existence potentially undermines everyone else's belief in the organisation's sincerity and commitment, because they provide targets for the whole organisation's efforts to be belittled and because they can potentially consume a lot of time, effort and money while still doing a poor job.

So senior management attention here is focused on non-performance, defining it as unacceptable and requiring good active support as a non-negotiable part of the job. This is accomplished both by providing extra help and by reviewing the values and competence of staff (especially people who should be providing practice leadership) and, if necessary, dismissing them or moving them to different kinds of jobs where they can make some other contribution. These staff are likely to resist, and the organisation and its leaders may have to be prepared to spend a considerable amount of time and effort to resolve the matter.

Broadly speaking, McLean's approach is an example of the change strategy called 'logical incrementalism' (Quinn 1980), which conceptualises the change process as one of iterative adjustment towards a broadly defined goal, learning from experience along the way and drawing people from all levels of the organisation (and, in this case, from the people being served, their families and advocates). It contrasts with top-down planning where the entire sequence of steps is mapped at the outset and then more or less rigidly implemented down through the organisation. This approach is arguably never practicable, and in human services, where there is much greater variability and unpredictability, especially unlikely to succeed. Thus, in understanding Figure 6.1, it is important to recognise that this coherent plan was derived in an incremental way and not simply imposed from the top of the organisation.

It is also important to say (as Ian McLean would) that this sequence of stages is not as simple and straightforward as presented here. There are likely to be setbacks along the way and periods when there are only 'moments of excellence' to be celebrated, with the recognition that there is a longer journey ahead. But all progress is worthwhile, both in terms of the direct benefit to the person with intellectual disabilities and because it demonstrates again what it is possible for people to achieve if they are supported well. It is not necessary to be perfect to start, but it is possible for people to make a difference from the beginning, even though much remains to be done.

Monitoring and evaluating performance

It should be obvious from what has been written so far that monitoring and evaluating performance is a central factor in determining the success of attempts to introduce active support. Monitoring the wrong things – in particular, monitoring administrative processes – risks communicating to staff that these are what matter most.

In the most successful organisations, senior managers and anyone else who is interested (family members, advocates, trustees, inspectors, funders) can see for themselves that active support is being provided to good effect. When they visit people receiving support, they find people engaged in meaningful activities to their evident interest and enjoyment. People are being supported to take part to the greatest extent possible, irrespective of their degree of intellectual disability or other problems they may have. The activities take place at home and in the community, and involve relationships with other people as much as tasks or events. The choice of activities, and how they unfold, is controlled as much as possible by the individual.

The team members providing support are using their skills discreetly, enabling the person they are supporting to do as much as he or she can. They can explain what they are doing and why and what difference it makes to the individual. When things are not going well, they change the way they are providing support and they do not rely on the typical excuses that people are too disabled, too challenging, are 'choosing' extensive disengagement, that the activities are not sufficiently 'valued' or that their own preferences are more important (Mansell et al. 2005). They can talk credibly, with examples, about how they have learned to provide better active support and how they work as a team to sustain good practice.

For the team, having people comment knowledgeably and supportively about their work indicates that it is important. Being able to discuss obstacles and difficulties with senior managers visiting helps people feel that their concerns are being understood and listened to.

The point is that if active support is being provided well, it will be obvious and visible to anyone who cares to look. As a management monitoring strategy, this is 'management by walking about' (Peters and Waterman 1982, pp.122, 288 et seq.). In our view, it is the most important method of monitoring and supporting good practice. Direct experience of what is really happening in the lives of people receiving support provides a rich agenda for management meetings and decision making.

Most organisations do also need to quantify more precisely how well they are doing. The experience of Mansell et al. (1994), referred to in Chapter 1, in which managers, taught to undertake routine observational data collection, reported a rising trend but independent observations found no change, has made us cautious about expecting managers to make use of the same methods as researchers. Such methods require skill and attention to detail that may be more difficult for managers to adopt, given the many other demands of their job. In the most recent training materials, simple rating scales are suggested as an alternative. In practice, most organisations we have worked with have preferred to pay for regular evaluation with an independent component, using the kind of observational methods in the published research. In most cases, the practice development team responsible for training and advice collects some observational data, with independent evaluators helping with data collection, inter-observer agreement and data analysis.

As an example of this Mansell et al. (2011) explored the quality of life and quality of support in six Australian organisations – all at different stages of implementing active support, using different approaches, methods and trainers. Baseline observations of a sample of houses in each organisation were collected. Across the six organisations, it initially appeared that there were similar levels of performance (see Figure 6.2). Engagement levels were on average quite high (52%), but average ABS for this sample was also higher than in many other studies (mean ABS Part 1 score=153). There were, on average, very low levels of assistance (3%) and other contact from staff (10%). This implies that people were engaging, without support, in activities that either were so simple that people could do them without support (such as listening to personal music players or watching television), or which did not require support because the person has many skills and just needed the opportunity or permission to engage.

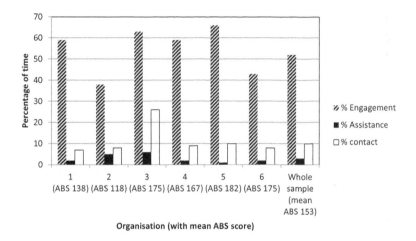

Figure 6.2 Mean percentage of time in engagement, assistance and contact for the Mansell *et al.* (2011) sample

However, selecting only the most severely disabled – people with ABS scores less than 151 (that is, below 50% of maximum ABS scores), there was a very different picture; only in one organisation is active support being delivered and there it appears to be having dramatic results. Figures 6.3, 6.4, 6.5 and 6.6 illustrate the findings. As can be seen, Organisation 3 was the only organisation providing good active support – that is, active support measure percentage scores above 67. Although the small numbers of people with ABS less than 151 in some of the organisations makes statistical analysis unwise (only Organisation 2 included more than ten people in this more severely disabled group), it is clear from the graphs that outcomes for individuals in Organisation 3 were substantially better. Whether or not it is statistically significant, a minimum difference in average engagement of almost 40 per cent is likely to have a socially and clinically significant effect on the quality of life of the people supported. People in Organisation 3 were also receiving more contact from staff than in any other organisation, including assistance.

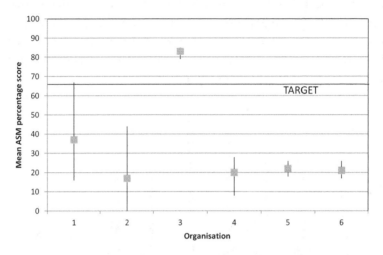

Figure 6.3 Active support scores (mean and range) across six organisations for people with ABS scores less than 151, at initial assessment[2]

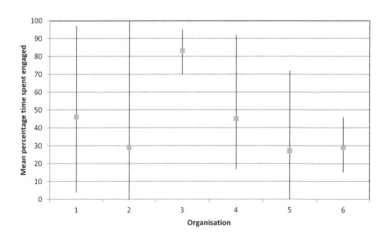

Figure 6.4 Engagement in meaningful activity and relationships (mean and range) across services in six organisations providing support to people with ABS scores less than 151

2   For Figures 6.3–6.6, the number in each organisation was as follows: Organisation 1–10 people; Organisation 2–23 people; Organisation 3–3 people; Organisation 4–5 people; Organisation 5–4 people; and Organisation 6–5 people.

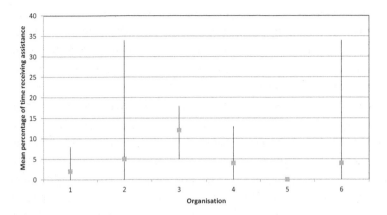

Figure 6.5 Assistance (mean and range) from staff across services in six organisations providing support to people with ABS scores less than 151

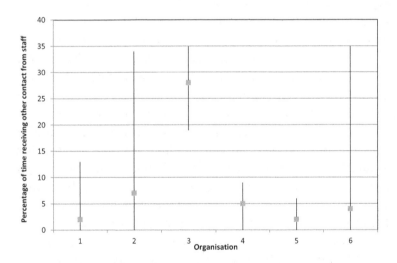

Figure 6.6 Other contact from staff (mean and range) across services in six organisations providing support to people with ABS scores less than 151

This example illustrates the importance of looking at the relationship between severity of disability, provision of active support and engagement in meaningful activity and relationships. Clearly, Organisation 3 was being much more successful in implementing active support than any of the other five, though all organisations believed they were succeeding.

The importance of sustained management focus is a lesson United Response drew from their regular audits. The 2008 audit showed that engagement and active support had decreased since 2005. In trying to work out why this might have been the case, the senior managers of the organisation and the practice development team identified the introduction of a new initiative as having distracted attention from active support. The organisation had introduced person-centred thinking training and person-centred thinking tools (Sanderson and Smull 2011) for supervision, team meetings and person-centred planning processes, and much effort and emphasis had gone into that across the organisation. Staff reported using the tools and appeared to have quite a good understanding of person-centred thinking but in practice were not using person-centred active support as much as they needed to. Inadvertently, the organisation appeared to have given the message to staff that active support was less important because they were using person-centred thinking.

In response to the findings from the audit, the organisation began a series of activities to refocus staff and managers on active support and to emphasise that person-centred thinking was a tool to help them put person-centred active support into practice (part of 'The Way We Work'), not an alternative activity. In addition, more managers were given practice leadership training and more person-centred active support training. The next two years' audits have demonstrated that the original levels had been regained. Attention is now focused on those teams that seem to be 'coasting' – not improving the quality of active support they are providing and therefore not achieving the quality of life that the best services are now routinely achieving.

The process of review, intervention and review is a permanent part of the work of the service. Changing demands from external agencies, changes in the nature of the support needed as people become more or less independent and, above all, changes in personnel mean that there is always work to do to sustain a good level of support.

Conclusion

In the first part of this chapter, the research literature on factors influencing care practices such as active support was reviewed and showed that there was no single factor or set of factors that provided a simple explanation for good practice. Those leading organisations supporting people with intellectual disabilities therefore have to adopt the principles of good leadership and management to make active support happen. In truth, these principles – a clear vision articulated from the top of the organisation, carried through in every aspect of its work, attending both to the skills and to the motivation of staff – are not different from those which any organisation has to adopt to succeed.

What seems to make life especially difficult for organisations providing support to people with severe or profound intellectual disabilities, and the staff who work in them, is that the external environment in which they operate is itself unclear about what they should achieve. Nowhere have we found clear support for services to improve the quality of support they offer to the people with severe or profound intellectual disabilities they serve. Funding agencies seem concerned mainly with cost reduction and managing demand for services, often responding to crises rather than in any planned way. Regulators (inspectors or others who have a quality control function) usually seem to focus on minimum standards which do not distinguish between services that provide good support and those that do not. In both cases, these important external influences may be sympathetic to improving the quality of support but they see their primary interest as lying elsewhere.

The directors and leaders of support-providing organisations can try to protect their staff from these influences, both by trying to manage external demands and, where possible, to renegotiate them so that they at least do not hinder the provision of good support. The repeated demonstration that active support has good results in enabling people with severe or profound intellectual disabilities to grow in independence, control and inclusion strengthens the case for it in the context of evidence-based policy making. The tenacity of organisations and their staff who do their best in spite of these obstacles creates a potential lobby to influence government and the wider field.

CHAPTER 7

Integrating Active Support with Other Person-Centred Approaches

Aligning different management and organisational processes so that they provide consistent help to implement active support, both practically and through communicating a clear message about its priority, seems logical and important. One specific area in which this needs to be done is in the range of working methods that are promoted among services for people with intellectual disabilities. These are the particular contribution of specialist intellectual disability services, depending on knowledge about intellectual and developmental disabilities and experience of intervention. The most important examples are:

- person-centred planning (O'Brien and O'Brien 2000)

- positive behaviour support (Carr *et al.* 1999; Koegel, Koegel and Dunlap 1996)

- total communication (Jones 2000)

- intensive interaction (Nind and Hewett 1994)

- the National Autistic Society's SPELL framework (see p.163) for supporting people on the autistic spectrum (Beadle-Brown and Mills 2010).

Like active support, each of these is presented as good practice for people providing support to individuals with severe or profound intellectual disabilities, backed by research (at least to some extent), and there are training materials available and experts promoting their use.

The existence of several approaches – and there are others less well supported by research too, such as facilitated communication (Biklen 1993; Felce 1994) and gentle teaching (McGee *et al.* 1987; Mudford 1995) – has unfortunately often led services and their staff to treat them as a menu, from which to select what seems the most relevant or is the most fashionable or heavily promoted. Thus people say, 'We don't do active support because we do intensive interaction' (for example, see Ashman *et al.* 2010, p.151).

This overlooks two important issues. First, some of these approaches are complementary. For example, intensive interaction is a method of establishing a relationship with a person with profound intellectual and multiple disabilities – a relationship that is necessary if the person is going to be supported to engage in meaningful activity and that will need active support to enable it to develop and flourish. Person-centred planning is a way of charting the longer-term goals and plans a person has; it is likely to need good active support to help identify which goals are the right ones and to enable the person to achieve these goals. Second, active support is actually a component of these approaches. For example, an early step in positive behaviour support is to ensure that people have good support to enable them to participate in activities they like (Risley 1996); active support is the way in which people with severe or profound intellectual disabilities can achieve this. The SPELL framework (see p.163) includes structured approaches to increase the predictability and consistency of activity and expectations, together with positive approaches to involving people in activity and relationships – both characteristics of active support.

Thus, the five approaches listed above need to be seen as complementary to active support rather than as alternatives to it. In this chapter, we describe each approach in turn, briefly reviewing the evidence for its effectiveness and then identifying how it fits together with active support. At the end, we illustrate how two organisations, United Response and Golden City Support Services, draw different approaches together in a way that attempts to provide staff with an integrated, coherent view of how they should be providing support.

Person-centred planning

Person-centred planning is an approach to organising assistance to people with intellectual disabilities, developed over more than 30 years in the United States of America, and influential in many other countries. It is a family of approaches and techniques (Mount and Zwernik 1988; Pearpoint, O'Brien and Forest 1993; Sanderson, Kennedy and Ritchie 1996; Smull and Burke-Harrison 1992; Vandercook, York and Forest 1989) which share certain characteristics (O'Brien and O'Brien 2000) rather than a single, codified approach. It is individualised, in that it is intended to reflect the unique circumstances of the individual person with intellectual disabilities both in assessing and in organising what should be done. It shares this focus with earlier approaches to individualised planning adopted in intellectual disability services, such as individual programme plans (Accreditation Council on Services for Mentally Retarded and Other Developmentally Disabled Persons 1983; Blunden 1980; Houts and Scott 1975; Jenkins et al. 1988) or individual service plans (Brost et al. 1982; Emerson et al. 1987), as well as with case management methods adopted across many client groups (Challis and Davies 1986).

What makes person-centred planning different from these approaches, however, is that it emphasises three other characteristics:

- It aims to consider aspirations and capacities expressed by the disabled person or those speaking on his or her behalf, rather than needs and deficiencies. Person-centred planning emphasises the authority of the individual person's voice, reflecting dissatisfaction with the perceived failure of professionals to attend to what matters most to service users, the extent to which services are seen to constrain or impose goals and the way in which services sometimes create artificial hurdles between goals in an inappropriate 'readiness model' or 'developmental continuum' (Crocker 1990; O'Brien and Lovett 1992; Taylor 1988; Wilcox and Bellamy 1987b).

- It tries to include and mobilise the individual's family and wider social network, as well as to use resources from the system of statutory services. This partly reflects the special interest that family and friends have and the idea that families have a stake in the arrangements made to support an individual with intellectual disabilities in a way that service employees do not (Sanderson 2000). Mobilising the person's social network is also intended to broaden and deepen the range of resources available to help him or her; indeed, for some authors there is the suggestion that services are part of the problem more than they are part of the solution (O'Brien and Lovett 1992, p.13). The social network is seen as a richer source of imagination, creativity and resources than the service system.

- It emphasises providing the support required to achieve goals, rather than limiting goals to what services typically can manage. Instead of making people wait because they lack skills (the 'readiness model'), person-centred planning is based on a 'support model', which provides whatever support is needed to achieve the goals people have (Sanderson 2000).

Although methods differ in detail, the general approach to person-centred planning is that a facilitator works with a 'circle of support' to develop a plan of how the person's life should unfold over the medium to long term. The circle of support is drawn from those who know the person well, care about him or her and who have a long-term interest in him or her. Ideally, it will include family and friends, rather than being dominated by professionals. The facilitator will, ideally, not be drawn from the staff providing services to the individual. The scope of the plan is not restricted to specific areas (such as an individual education plan or an individual health plan) but focuses on the individual's own priorities, whatever they are. The time-frame is months and years, and the questions considered include big questions about the course of the person's life rather than just focusing on short-term goals.

Of course, although the language of person-centred planning implies that the individual being supported is weighing the options and making the decisions, for many people with severe or profound intellectual disabilities this will only be true to a limited extent. Those around the person will often be trying to interpret, from what they know of the individual, what is the best thing to do, using whatever legal frameworks are in force to guide decision making where the person does not have legal capacity. The basis for these decisions, and who has the mandate to make them, differs in different places and is often complex and difficult for families and support workers to understand. The language of personal control is a fiction intended to remind everyone else that the individual should be supported to make decisions to the greatest extent possible, and that the contribution of others should be in the person's interests.

The evidence base for person-centred planning is surprisingly limited. In our critique of UK policy (Mansell and Beadle-Brown 2004a, 2004b), we said:

> case studies suggest that person-centred planning can be valuable and may change the perception of participants. There are no good-quality, systematic evaluations of person-centred planning, but since person-centred planning shares many characteristics with previous attempts at individual planning evidence from these is relevant. This evidence suggests that when implemented on a large scale, there are problems with coverage, quality and outcomes. (Mansell and Beadle-Brown 2004a, p.4)

Robertson et al. (2005) concluded that 'despite the existence of a considerable amount of literature advocating the use of PCP, very little quantitative evidence exists with regard to the effectiveness of PCP in improving quality of life related outcomes' (p.9). Their own study of 65 people with a person-centred plan showed evidence of statistically significant gains in the number of people in individuals' social networks, their contact with friends and family, their involvement in community activities and scheduled day services and in the amount of choice they had over what they did. They found negative effects in more perceived risks, more reported health problems and more emotional and behavioural difficulties. Overall, they concluded that person-centred planning was:

> helpful but not enough in itself to promote social inclusion and that additional action to complement improved planning with individuals would be necessary. Such action is likely to include, for example, positive action to remove barriers to employment and mainstream housing options

and to encourage specialist services to play a stronger role
in enabling more inclusive social networks. (Robertson *et al.*
2005, p.105)

Nevertheless, person-centred planning has a strong policy, professional
and advocacy mandate in many jurisdictions in the USA and Canada
and is being adopted in Europe and Australasia. In the UK, the White
Papers *Valuing People* (Department of Health 2001b) and *Valuing
People Now* (Department of Health 2007b) identified person-centred
planning as a central tool for service reform, and detailed guidance
was issued (Department of Health 2001a).

We were critical of the policy as developed in the UK (Mansell
and Beadle-Brown 2004a, 2004b) because we believed that it risked
using scarce resources to write plans instead of change lives, and that
the plans produced would not be grounded in a real appreciation of
the possibilities and potential if individuals were not being supported
to do as much as possible for themselves. There has not yet been any
further evaluation of the number or quality of person-centred plans
against which to judge these criticisms. However, there is a trend in
recent writing about person-centred planning to move away from the
idea of a resource-intensive plan developed at the outset, in favour of
an iterative process of goal setting and review:

> For people being supported by services, it is not person
> centred planning that matters as much as the pervasive
> presence of person centred thinking. If people who use
> services are to have positive control over their lives, if they
> are to have self directed lives within their own communities
> then those who are around the person, especially those who
> do the day to day work need to have person centred thinking
> skills. Only a small percentage of people need to know how
> to write good person centred plans, but everyone involved
> needs to have good skills in person centred thinking, in the
> value based skills that underlie the planning. (Sanderson
> and Smull 2011, p.1)

Thus the criticism that person-centred planning uses up resources
to produce plans which may then not be implemented may be less
important in future.

How do person-centred planning and person-centred active support fit together? Mansell *et al.* proposed that:

> Done well, person-centred planning gives a sense of a longer-term direction in a person's life, provides the 'bigger picture' about what the person wants and how to get there, and mobilises interest and enthusiasm to make progress. (2005, p.149)

This sense of strategic direction is important and not necessarily likely to arise out of the everyday experience of life. There are many situations where services focus on everyday questions of how they could provide support to enable people to do different activities, or meet new people, or get on better with the people they know, where the more important question is 'Why is this person living here?' or 'What does this person really want to do with his or her life?' Although other people do not necessarily have a person-centred plan, many people do have a sense of the broad direction they would like their life to follow – the career they want to pursue, where they want to live, the kind of lifestyle they want – and that is what a good person-centred plan should provide.

A similar point is made by Harman and Sanderson (2008) who argue that, in the absence of person-centred planning, longer-term goals are derived from sources such as individual programme plans which may focus much more on services than on the individual's quality of life.

Active support, then, provides a primary means of achieving goals in the person-centred plan. Sometimes other things will be needed too – if the goal is to get a new home somewhere else, then much of that has nothing particular to do with active support – but often active support will be important. For example, if one of the goals someone has is to get a gardening job and the first steps towards this are that the person does some voluntary work with a conservation team, then active support will be needed to ensure that the person gets on well with the other volunteers and is able to make a successful contribution to the work. In this sense, active support is one of a number of possible ways in which the goals of the person-centred plan are realised (Mansell *et al.* 2005, p.149; Sanderson, Jones and Brown 2002).

However, active support makes another contribution to good person-centred planning. Identifying important personal goals with people who often have impoverished backgrounds, impaired communication and limited ability to imagine and discuss opportunities they have not experienced is a difficult task. These obstacles are widespread among the population of people with severe or profound intellectual disabilities (Mansell and Beadle-Brown 2004b). Identifying personal preferences, individual strengths and weaknesses and potential avenues for growth and development is likely to be easier if it is based on experience of enabling the person to take part in different activities and relationships:

> Person-centred active support helps inform plans about individual strengths, possible directions and aspirations, grounded in the reality of working with the individual. Only when the 'circle of support' helping to organise a person-centred plan know the person well enough can they help make realistic goals and achieve progress. Knowing the person is much easier if it is based on a real relationship that involves practical help to engage in meaningful activity and relationships. You learn much more by supporting people to do things than by sitting with them while they do nothing. (Mansell *et al.* 2005, p.149)

Thus, we would argue that providing active support to enable people to broaden their experience and have some success at trying new things might be a better place to start person-centred planning than holding a meeting to guess what people's aspirations might be. We would not, therefore, support the view expressed by Harman and Sanderson (2008) who argue that writing a person-centred plan should always precede a move to providing active support. For us, active support would be part of the 'continual listening and learning' that Sanderson (2000) defines as characteristic of person-centred planning.

Thus, person-centred planning and person-centred active support ought at least to be complementary processes, each informing the other; arguably, it is not possible to do either well without the other.

Positive behaviour support

Positive behaviour support (Carr *et al.* 2002, 1999) grew out of dissatisfaction with the way ideas, developed in the field of behaviour analysis, were being applied in practice in response to challenging behaviour. Early applications of behavioural methods often focused on eliminating problem behaviour without thinking about what should replace it (Winett and Winkler 1972), and used aversive methods that, though powerful, often had unintended side effects and raised ethical questions (Goldiamond 1974). Positive behaviour support is characterised by:

- a focus on building constructive behaviours and a good lifestyle for the individual; what is called *a constructional approach* (Goldiamond 1974; Risley 1996)

- intervention based on assessment of the function or purposes of the challenging behaviour (Carr 1977; O'Neill *et al.* 1990)

- paying attention to altering and enriching the environment in which problems occur, to remove triggers and promote constructive or adaptive behaviour (Emerson, McGill and Mansell 1994; Koegel *et al.* 1996; Luiselli and Cameron 1998)

- helping individuals to develop their ability to communicate and to participate in activities so that they have less need to resort to challenging behaviour (Carr and Durand 1985; LaVigna, Willis and Donellan 1989).

- the role of reinforcement becoming complementary, given these proactive, preventative approaches; positive behaviour support uses non-aversive methods (LaVigna and Donellan 1986).

Thus, as Carr *et al.* explain, positive behaviour support is:

> the construction of a comprehensive set of procedures that include change of the environment to make problem behaviors irrelevant, instruction on appropriate behaviors that makes the problem behavior inefficient, and manipulation of consequences to ensure that appropriate behaviors are more consistently and powerfully reinforced than are problem behaviors. (1999, p.4)

The 'comprehensive set of procedures' might well include broad arrangements such as where individuals live and with whom, what they have to do during the day, as well as the way support is provided by staff.

The components of positive behaviour support have been extensively researched and have strong empirical support (Carr *et al.* 1999). Evaluation of services based on positive behaviour support principles also show good results (Kincaid *et al.* 2002; Mansell *et al.* 2001; Toogood 2000; Toogood *et al.* 2011). Positive behaviour support therefore has a growing policy, professional and advocacy mandate in the USA, Canada, the UK and Australasia. However, as with person-centred planning, the results achieved in demonstration projects are not necessarily matched by routine practice in the field and this is recognised in much of the policy guidance (American Association on Intellectual and Developmental Disabilities and ARC of the United States 2010; Department of Health 1993, 2007a; Queensland Government 2007).

It should be clear from the description given above that positive behaviour support is not a 'treatment' for the individual whose behaviour presents a challenge, delivered by a specialist in some kind of clinic. Its focus on improving the environment, helping the individual develop new skills and improving the person's quality of life mean that it involves everyone providing support to the individual, in every aspect of the person's life. And that is its connection with active support. Good active support involves enabling the individual, even if he or she has additional problems such as challenging behaviour, to participate in the activities and relationships of everyday life. It is therefore a fundamental building block of positive behaviour support. It would not be possible to provide positive behaviour support without providing active support.

Total communication

Many people with severe or profound intellectual disabilities have difficulties expressing themselves or understanding what other people are saying to them. For example, a study of adults living in group homes in England (Mansell *et al.* 2002a) found that 43 per cent had major communication difficulties and 63 per cent had impaired social interaction. There is evidence that staff often misjudge the receptive language ability of people with intellectual disabilities (Bradshaw 2001; McConkey, Morris and Purcell 1999; Purcell, Morris and McConkey 1999), a common error being to rely too heavily on verbal communication. As outlined in the SPELL framework (see p.163), it is also considered good practice when supporting people with autism to reduce reliance on verbal communication and use visual methods to promote understanding and expression – exclusive use of verbal methods of communication excludes and disables people with autism spectrum conditions, whereas use of visual methods plays to their strengths (Beadle-Brown and Mills 2010). Similarly, the extent to which people with intellectual disabilities can understand choices and decisions is often limited and requires careful assessment (Arscott, Dagnan and Kroese 1999; Murphy and Clare 1995).

It is, therefore, not surprising that many people with intellectual disabilities are extremely socially isolated. Studies of people in residential settings, for example, often show low levels of contact from other staff and other residents, particularly for people with severe and profound intellectual disabilities (Emerson and Hatton 1994; Felce and Perry 1995; Mansell 1994). Studies of the social networks of people with intellectual disabilities show that they are often extremely restricted and dominated by family and staff. Cambridge et al. (2001) found that, on average, people living in the community 12 years after deinstitutionalisation had very limited social networks compared with the wider population. They found that only 19 per cent of members of these networks were unrelated to intellectual disability services. Robertson et al. (2001) found even smaller networks. Forrester-Jones et al. (2004) found that people attending a supported employment programme had networks averaging fewer than 50 people and nearly two-thirds of network members were staff, family or other service users.

Given the importance of communication and the evident need for help, 'total communication' is a method that draws together all available methods of communication and augmented and alternative communication (speech, signing, gestures, symbols, pictures, objects of reference, communication passports, body language), teaches people providing support to be sensitive to all of these as methods of communication and then derives individualised schemes using methods that people can use in their own situation to communicate with those around them (Jones 2000).

Although the individual components or strategies of augmented and alternative communication have often been evaluated, there is much less research on total communication as an integrated approach (for example, Brandford 2008; Bunning 2008; Jago, Jago and Hart 1984) and less of a mandate from policy makers to support it.

For active support, effective communication is essential. Active support training materials emphasise the importance of not just relying on speech but using the positioning of materials and body language to 'make the situation speak for itself' (Mansell *et al.* 2005, p.55). Where the individual being supported uses particular augmented and alternative communication strategies, part of providing *person-centred* active support is to understand and use them too. For total communication, the value of active support is that activity and relationships provide the substrate for communication – something interesting to talk about and a reason to try and communicate. Thus, total communication is not an alternative to active support; they are complementary approaches which will often need to be used together.

Intensive interaction

Intensive interaction is different from each of the other examples of person-centred approaches given in this chapter. They are all concerned with ongoing processes designed to support people with severe or profound intellectual disabilities in various aspects of their lives. Intensive interaction is not intended as an ongoing process but as a specific intervention to build rapport and a relationship with a person whose social behaviour is extremely limited.

> The paradigm underlying Intensive Interaction is that of the Infant-Mother interaction, in which the infant initiates a sound or movement or rhythm and the mother responds in an imitative way. Once the baby's initiative is sufficiently confirmed they are able to move on and try out something else. It is crucial to emphasise that in using Intensive Interaction we are not in any way infantilising our conversation partners, since for all of us, this non-verbal dialogue is a primary communication pathway, laid down

in babyhood but remaining with us all our lives. (Caldwell 2011)

Essentially, then, intensive interaction involves imitating noises or movements the person with intellectual disabilities makes, so that he or she learns that his or her behaviour produces a response from the person providing support. The expectation is that, over time, the individual becomes more comfortable with the person providing support and more likely to initiate interaction, and will use a wider range of methods of interacting.

Intensive interaction has been promoted particularly for use with people with profound intellectual and multiple disabilities (Hewett and Nind 1998; Nind and Hewett 1994, 2001; Samuel et al. 2008) and also people on the autistic spectrum who are very socially withdrawn (Caldwell 2006, 2007, 2008). It has a limited evidence base, dominated by case studies relying mainly on qualitative measures (for example, Kellett 2005; Watson and Fisher 1997) but there are also some small-scale quantitative studies demonstrating increased sociability and interaction (Leaning and Watson 2006; Nind 1996; Samuel et al. 2008).

There is an obvious similarity between intensive interaction and active support, in that both are designed to coax people into engaging in activities and relationships through encouragement and success. Where people are extremely withdrawn or seem to have no interest in interaction, intensive interaction provides a way to begin that process (Ashman et al. 2010, pp.173–5). One reservation expressed about intensive interaction is that the imitative activities might seem childish and therefore in conflict with the general desire to use age-appropriate activities and situations (Firth et al. 2008). This seems to be a question of balance and pragmatism: the desire not to represent people with severe or profound intellectual disabilities as like little children is probably not compromised by occasional activities that might look childlike. The benefits of showing a person hitherto non-communicative and withdrawn as being sociable and interested probably outweigh any such risk.

The SPELL framework

The SPELL framework has been developed by the National Autistic Society over the past 50 years of working with children and adults on the autism spectrum, their families and those who support and teach them. It is described by Beadle-Brown and Mills (2010) as a framework for supporting children and adults on the autism spectrum which uses person-centred, socially valid approaches to reduce the more disabling effects of autism, encourage and promote the strengths of autism and overall improve quality of life. It is not a one-size-fits-all programme but a framework to help people work out what might be needed to make life better for the individual they support. It is considered to be the foundation on to which other approaches and interventions can be built.

SPELL is an acronym and stands for:

- Structure

- Positive approaches and expectations

- Empathy

- Low arousal

- Links.

Structure

Structure involves the use of supports such as visual timetables, environmental management and other non-verbal communication aids, to make the world more comprehensible and predictable and thus reduce anxiety. Of course, it is important to do this in a person-centred way, using the methods that work best for each individual. As already discussed in Chapter 4, using structure – in particular, visual structure – is a good way of increasing predictability and helping people to understand what is needed in an activity or what will happen during the day. It is also a way of providing graded assistance and reducing the need for staff prompts, thus avoiding prompt dependency and increasing independence.

Structure is not the same as rigid routine. It does not mean that people have to do the same thing every day, nor does it mean that they cannot try new things or that everyone has to do the same thing. It is important to build change into people's routines in order to encourage flexibility but in a carefully managed way to avoid anxiety. Normative aids to structure such as diaries, calendars, electronic devices or notes provide the same function, and using more elaborate aids that work best for autistic individuals is just an extension of what we expect in our own lives.

Structure forms a major part of other intervention approaches such as TEACCH (Mesibov *et al.* 2004) and although some of the evaluative research has had methodological issues (Jordan and Jones 1999), the evidence overall is that structured teaching and approaches appear to be effective in reducing challenging behaviour, improving communication and social interaction, improving sensorimotor skills and independence both with children and adults (Mesibov 1997; Ozonoff and Cathcart 1998; Panerai *et al.* 1998; Panerai, Ferrante and Zingale 2002; Person 2000; Sapieras and Beadle-Brown 2006; Schopler *et al.* 1981).

Positive approaches and expectations

'Positive approaches and expectations' is described by Beadle-Brown and Mills (2010) as supporting people to try new things safely, so they can make choices, learn and grow in independence, rather than allowing people to sit and do nothing or to engage in self-stimulatory behaviour all the time because they seem to be 'choosing' to do so. In essence, positive approaches are concerned with engaging people in meaningful activities and relationships with a helpful style of interaction that is embedded in positive attitudes and a knowledge of the individual, essentially using person-centred active support, total communication and positive behaviour support.

Positive approaches is also about playing to people's strengths, working with people to find the skills that they already have and then helping them to develop their strengths, to achieve their maximum potential. This means having high enough expectations that people do not become bored and therefore resort to self-stimulatory or self-injurious behaviour, but not such high expectations that people are paralysed by anxiety and lack of confidence. It is also about valuing their contribution, whatever that might be.

Finally, positive approaches is about how we portray people with autism to others – the language and imagery used, the places provided for them to live in, the way they are introduced and presented to new people, the activities offered to them (age-appropriate and real), and the way they are supported to be valued members of their community. This echoes the positive imagery and symbolism emphasised in social role valorisation (Flynn and Lemay 1999; Wolfensberger 2000).

Empathy

It is important to be able to empathise with individuals and find ways to understand their perspective – even though they may not be able to communicate this directly. Good observation and listening skills and a thorough assessment are all important. In order to understand the perspective of individuals, it is necessary to assess the functions of behaviour, level of comprehension and understanding and the sensory issues experienced by them. It is important to get to know them and to share this knowledge widely with those involved in their lives so that everyone understands what interests or bores them, what may upset or frighten them, what they find comfortable, uncomfortable and so on. Many people with autism experience the world in very different ways from other people and it is important to understand how each individual is affected by his or her autism or disability.

Empathy is not about acknowledging the difficulties people face and then allowing them to avoid any difficult situation but about supporting them through those difficulties using rehearsal of potentially difficult scenarios, positive approaches and expectations and structure. The SPELL framework is not about finding one 'autism-friendly approach' for all people with autism spectrum conditions but the right approach to support each individual.

Low arousal

This element of the framework applies to both the environment and the way staff and other people interact with an individual. Ensuring a low-arousal environment is important to improve focus and concentration, but it is also important in reducing anxiety and managing 'challenging behaviour'.

It is generally accepted that the sensory profile of individuals with autism frequently differs markedly from that of the general population and that they may be either over- or under-sensitive across the full range of sensory domains (Kern et al. 2006). They may be sensitive to light, sound, heat and touch. They may have problems integrating the various sensory domains into a coherent whole. Displays of what might be seen as challenging behaviour may be a reaction to these and an attempt to regulate and achieve equilibrium. It is here that attention to interaction and environment is crucial.

Beadle-Brown and Mills (2010) point out that any low-arousal approaches need to be person-centred since what brings about a state of high arousal can be very different for different people. This links back to the importance of empathy – being aware of how the environment affects each individual should dictate how best to arrange his or her environment. In terms of interactions, it is important to use a quiet, non-confrontational approach with individuals with autism. Confrontation is one of the most commonly occurring and most easily avoided causes of challenging behaviour and rapidly escalates levels of stress and arousal.

Low arousal is not the same as no arousal. Giving people the opportunity to experience new and potentially anxiety-provoking events or activities little and often, with control over the course of the activity as described in Chapter 3, will help people to be able to engage in activities and interactions in the future (Carr and Collins 1992; Marvin 1998).

Links

This element of the framework is primarily focused on achieving consistency and predictability by enhancing communication between supporters and agencies in order to promote and support activities that are as socially inclusive as possible. Chapter 4 looked at this issue in detail with regard to how consistency and predictability can be achieved within a staff team. However, there is also a need to create links with the wider support network and the community. This is achieved through a partnership with families, schools, colleges, public agencies and so on, and it is here, often at times of transition, that things may go particularly badly. As noted in Chapter 4, there may be inconsistent methods of working, or key individuals may be left out when decisions are made. Those supporting people directly should not feel on their own or unsupported. They must be able to refer to others for advice, assessment, intervention and support. This may be particularly important where children and adults have more complex needs or challenging behaviour. Person-centred planning is a good example of how the links element of the framework can be achieved.

Integrating different approaches

The description of different person-centred approaches given above shows that they are complementary to active support, and that active support is in fact a component of them. Nevertheless, the idea that people providing support can pick and choose at will from what they see as a menu of alternatives is a potential problem. Providing an overarching account that integrates different approaches is therefore something organisations implementing active support have tried to do.

The SPELL framework is something of a hybrid in that it is explicitly a framework into which elements such as person-centred planning, positive behaviour support and person-centred active support can fit and also a specification of some more specific requirements such as providing a low-arousal environment.

Another example of this kind of framework comes from Golden City Support Services and was used in a strategic planning discussion by managers and directors in 2010. Figure 7.1 shows the overall framework, distinguishing the environment that the organisation operates in, the practice framework – how support is organised and delivered to achieve individual goals consistent with the mission of the organisation – and the way the organisation is organised to support delivery of the practice framework. Distinguishing these three arenas helps staff to see whether particular problems they face are something to do with the way they provide support, the way the organisation is organised or with the wider disability support system in which the organisation operates.

Overview

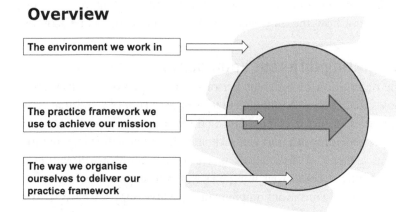

The environment we work in

The practice framework we use to achieve our mission

The way we organise ourselves to deliver our practice framework

Figure 7.1 Golden City Support Services framework

The environment we work in

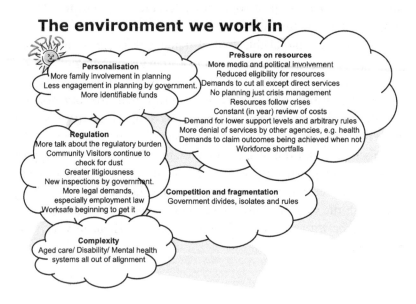

Personalisation
More family involvement in planning
Less engagement in planning by government.
More identifiable funds

Pressure on resources
More media and political involvement
Reduced eligibility for resources
Demands to cut all except direct services
No planning just crisis management
Resources follow crises
Constant (in year) review of costs
Demand for lower support levels and arbitrary rules
More denial of services by other agencies, e.g. health
Demands to claim outcomes being achieved when not
Workforce shortfalls

Regulation
More talk about the regulatory burden
Community Visitors continue to check for dust
Greater litigiousness
New inspections by government.
More legal demands, especially employment law
Worksafe beginning to get it

Competition and fragmentation
Government divides, isolates and rules

Complexity
Aged care/ Disability/ Mental health systems all out of alignment

Figure 7.2 Mapping the environment

The way we organise ourselves to deliver our practice framework

Better decision making and improved communication
Are the activities of managers invisible to staff?
When to share versus protect staff?
How does indecision/ lack of decision determine how staff perceive GCSS?
How does information 'trickle down' to all staff?
Are workers disempowered?
What is the effect of message 'we're not there yet' plus no performance data?
Various organisational processes are misunderstood, e.g. what is training?
Major changes likely in all programmes over next 5 years –
staff experiencing processes as uncertain and /or slow

Not enough evidence
to support service
delivery claims

Link focus on staff and mission
Staff are the vehicle
to a good life for
people we support

Do staff want to help?
Are staff demonstrating a desire to be more involved?
What opportunities are there for co-production?

Workload management
Finding the balance between
a sustainable organisation
and good service delivery

Figure 7.3 Using the practice framework to review what
the organisation does and needs to do better

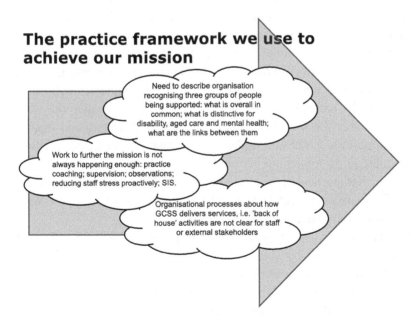

The practice framework we use to achieve our mission

Need to describe organisation
recognising three groups of people
being supported: what is overall in
common; what is distinctive for
disability, aged care and mental health;
what are the links between them

Work to further the mission is not
always happening enough: practice
coaching; supervision; observations;
reducing staff stress proactively; SIS.

Organisational processes about how
GCSS delivers services, i.e. 'back of
house' activities are not clear for staff
or external stakeholders

Figure 7.4 Issues encountered when describing the practice
framework used by Golden City Support Services

Figures 7.2–7.4 take each of these arenas and identify the major issues in each. So, for example, the environment is characterised by an explicit commitment to personalisation, but also by increasing pressure on costs and on regulation in a situation in which services are fragmented, complex and often in competition with each other. On the horizon is the prospect of an Australian National Disability Insurance Scheme which would double expenditure on disability services and provide a boost for personalisation (Productivity Commission 2011). Within this environment, the key issues facing Golden City (serving a dispersed, rural population) include communication and how support staff use their creativity and commitment to improve practice, without pretending that things are better than they are. These were the key issues identified by a group including finance, personnel and health and safety managers; the fact that they are focused on enabling staff reflects the success of Golden City's attempts, referred to in the previous chapter, to align organisational priorities.

For Golden City, three major issues emerge in describing the practice framework. First, this is an organisation serving people with different labels (and funded and regulated by different parts of the service system). Active support is reasonably well understood in disability services but not in aged care or mental health services. So one priority is to develop an account that works in these services, which draws on the best from each area of practice and which provides staff with a coherent story about what they do and why. Second, managers are concerned that they are not yet achieving implementation in a sufficiently consistent and thorough way. And, finally, they are anxious that the links between administrative processes and quality of support are not always understood, so that people assume it is not possible to do something because of 'the rules' when in fact it might be; or that (particularly for external stakeholders) lack of knowledge of the impact of administrative processes on quality of support leads to unnecessary conflict.

The second example of an integrating framework is 'The Way We Work', developed by United Response. Here the focus is explicitly on the practice framework. Figure 7.5 shows the diagram used to illustrate the approach. It has four components – being clear about the values that underpin United Response's work, listening to the person, organising to provide the support he or she wants and needs and reviewing how well support is being provided.

Figure 7.5

The component on *values* takes the main aim – encouraging individuals to plan for and take control of their lives – and spells out what this would mean in practice:

- involving people in making decisions about their lives and in everyday activities

- supporting people to engage in meaningful activity and relationships

- choosing the style and nature of support that people receive from staff and others.

The component on *listening* identifies different ways in which the voice of the person being supported can be heard. This might include saying directly what he or she wants, or doing so using augmented and alternative communication such as objects of reference or signs. It might include paying particular attention to communication strategies such as intensive interaction or recognising barriers to communication such as hearing loss. It might also include discussion with people who know the person well as to what he or she prefers (which could be part of a 'circle of support' doing person-centred planning but could also go on all the time outside of formal structures). This discussion might extend to reflecting about the person's experience of life in the past, to understand his or her preferences and the reasons for these. Listening could also involve trying opportunities consistently and for some time to establish the individual's preferences – not assuming that his or her initial response is set in stone.

The component on *organising* recognises that people and resources have to be brought together in a planned way to make real change in a person's life. This involves:

- keyworking and facilitation of person-centred planning
- practice leadership to coach and shape good support among team members
- teamwork to develop the quality of support staff offer
- training staff to provide good quality support to people
- setting goals to aim for and management of staff and resources to ensure that staff do provide the support needed
- sharing good practice among members of the staff team and in the wider community
- plans and aide-memoires such as activity plans, support profiles and staff rotas
- ensuring that administrative processes help rather than hinder good support.

Finally, the component on *reviewing* emphasises that there is a wide range of methods that help people in the service learn how to do better. These include collating information from different sources (e.g. from visits, working together, stories, photographs, videos, quality checking processes); using team meetings and supervision as a forum for feedback and for reviewing and agreeing practice; and making sure that reviews happen when they should and that people are clear what needs to change to improve the person's life.

Like the other job-aids or aides-memoire described in this book, 'The Way We Work' does not replace the work of thinking through how to provide person-centred support in practice. What it does do, though, is provide a common language and framework in which different things can be located and described in a coherent way. It also provides a symbolic assertion of unity – that all the different practices that go on in the organisation are part of a whole, which the people being supported should experience as consistent and comprehensive as well as effective. When challenged and asked to explain how different things fit together, managers in United Response can use 'The Way We Work' to do so, and ultimately it is likely to be the credibility of this explanation and the understanding on which it is based that is important, rather than the diagram.

Conclusion

Looking at the different person-centred approaches described in this chapter, one point worth noting is that they have a more limited basis in research than does active support. In a world where there is increasing emphasis on the evidence underpinning policy and practice, it is interesting to note that some working methods have been adopted and promoted on the basis of rather less evidence than exists for active support, and that active support has not been taken up as a key policy initiative in spite of a quite compelling evidence base. We return to this in the next chapter.

The different approaches described here are not incompatible with each other. In many respects, they complement each other, and in some cases at least, active support seems to be an integral part of other approaches (such as positive behaviour support). If those supporting individuals with severe or profound intellectual disabilities are to make sense of these different approaches, they need both to be able to work within the logic of the particular approach (so they need to understand enough about intensive interaction or active support or methods of person-centred planning) so that they can do it well, and to link the different approaches together in an overall framework that makes sense and into which particular components can be fitted as they are needed.

CHAPTER 8

Conclusion

Introduction

Earlier chapters have provided a description of active support, explaining why and how it has developed, and drawn attention to differences in emphasis and approach. The different components that characterise active support have been explored, bringing the available research together with the experience of academics and practitioners putting it into operation. The factors that seem to us to be important in successfully implementing active support have been identified.

This chapter draws together the main lessons to be learned by those trying to use active support to improve the quality of life of people with severe or profound intellectual disabilities. It also looks ahead to the future agenda for active support, both for organisations providing support to people with intellectual disabilities and for researchers evaluating and developing it.

Lessons to be learned

We argued in Chapter 2 that engagement in meaningful activity and relationships was an important indicator of quality of life. If people have a good quality of life, it will be possible to see this in the richness and variety of activities and relationships in which they are involved. However, it is important to distinguish between the outcome *quality of life* and the indicator *engagement in meaningful activity and relationships*. They are not the same. For example, the quality of life domain *interpersonal relations* includes the indicators of the individual's social network and family contact as well as the quality and number of interactions he or she has. Focusing on engagement addresses the interactions but not how many different people are involved and what their relationship is with the individual. Engagement is not the *only* thing that is important, but it is a *necessary* part of quality of life.

It will therefore often be necessary to ask questions about more than engagement to understand a person's quality of life. In our view, though, it will never be possible to ignore engagement.

Similarly, it is important to distinguish between engagement as a *measure* and engagement as an *indicator* of quality of life. The observational measures of engagement used in most studies do not distinguish between activities chosen by staff and those chosen or preferred by the people receiving support. This does not mean that choice and control are not important aspects of person-centred active support, just that other measures have to be used to assess the extent to which they are improved as engagement increases. Focusing only on increasing the amount of activity, because that is what is measured, misunderstands the goal of active support, which is to improve quality of life.

The relatively large number of studies of engagement reviewed in Chapter 2 showed that people with intellectual disabilities engage in meaningful activities to a lesser extent than the general population. People are spending long hours each day essentially doing nothing. This extensive inactivity has bad effects on their physical and mental health; it represents a lack of fulfilment of individual potential and it contributes to prejudice and discrimination about intellectual disability.

Over the more than 20 years that researchers have been studying the level of engagement in meaningful activity and relationships as an indicator of quality of life, there is no overall trend in the data. People with intellectual disabilities are not engaging more than they were, despite all the efforts there have been to change policy and practice during this period. It appears that, left to their own devices, services providing support to people with intellectual disabilities in the community are no better now at enabling people to participate in meaningful activities and relationships than they ever were.

In general, the more severe a person's intellectual disability, the lower their engagement level, so that those people with higher support needs are more at risk of the bad consequences of disengagement. However, examination of the results of all the studies undertaken shows wide variation within them. Thus, there are many examples in the research where people with lower support needs are recorded as largely disengaged, even though in general people with lower support needs are likely to be engaged to a greater extent. Similarly, engagement levels among people with higher support needs vary. The level of a person's disability is important, but it is clearly not the only thing that determines his or her ability to participate in life.

In Chapter 3, we argued that, for people with severe and profound intellectual disabilities, help from other people is a critical factor in determining whether they can take part in activities and relationships. Without good help, people will not be able to access or organise things to do; they will not be able to undertake them and they will experience failure and dissatisfaction. The most important feature of active support is the nature of the help provided to the person with severe or profound intellectual disabilities. We call this the 'enabling relationship' and see it as the core of active support.

The available research provides an impressive body of evidence demonstrating that active support is effective at enabling people to engage in meaningful activity and relationships. For people with higher support needs, the effect of active support is to compensate for this, so that people are able to engage at similar levels to people with less severe disabilities. Even for people with lower support needs, active support can help improve people's engagement, either by giving them the freedom to do things they already have the skill to do (where they do not need much assistance) or by extending the range of available activities to more complex, more interesting and more demanding things, where the assistance needed is more to do with planning and organising than doing the task.

The gap between weaker and stronger implementation of active support is also striking in the research. Active support needs to be provided well to have a worthwhile impact on quality of life. Its success therefore depends on the quality of its implementation. Although each person providing support to an individual with severe or profound intellectual disabilities can try to build an enabling relationship, success is likely to depend on teamwork, organisation and leadership, often in a service-providing organisation.

There is usually more than one person providing support to an individual with severe or profound intellectual disabilities, sometimes in a situation where support is being provided to several individuals. This means that the people providing support have to be coordinated. Coordination is required both to deliver consistent support in the best form for the individual and to ensure that support is provided when people need it. In Chapter 4 we argued that although written plans and protocols might be a useful prompt to team members as to how to organise themselves and how to provide support, they are unlikely to be sufficient. More important is the thinking and discussion between team members (and the person they are supporting, his or her advocates and family) about how best to provide the support the person needs and wants. This is likely to provide a deeper understanding than following a list of instructions.

Thus, good teamwork is the key to providing well-organised, consistent support. This involves the development of a shared vision of the goals of the team and also a shared philosophy of how team members provide support. It is maintained by norms or rules which provide team members with expectations about what they should do and support and reinforcement for doing it. This cannot, however, be left to chance. Given the evidence that teams often develop inappropriate, anti-therapeutic norms, the process of team building and management requires leadership. This places the team leader in a particularly important position, both as a source of technical knowledge and skill to provide the right kind of support and as someone who can facilitate the development of a strong team committed to the right things and ensure that this is maintained over time. This is the role we have called 'practice leadership'.

Practice leaders are the custodians of the vision of the team and its culture. Their role is not characterised by administrative control, in which the supervisor acts as a conduit for organisational policies and procedures down to team members who are just expected to do what they are told. Nor is it simply being one of the team – working alongside other members as if the team were a democracy in which their voice counted for nothing more than anyone else's. Instead, it is a distinctive leadership role in which the person has sufficient sapiential authority to guide his or her team, the skills of a teacher and mentor in order to develop the team and the ability to defend good practice against other pressures.

Despite the limited amount of research on practice leadership and its exploratory nature, it seems clear that practice leadership is a central issue in enabling people to provide good support for individuals with severe or profound intellectual disabilities. This raises questions about their training, career development and support, and also about how their time is to be protected for the important work they do from the many other responsibilities with which first-line managers have become encumbered.

Looking at the wider organisation, review of the published research showed that there was no single factor or set of factors that provided a simple explanation for good practice. Those leading organisations supporting people with intellectual disabilities therefore have to adopt the principles of good leadership and management to make active support happen. These principles – a clear vision articulated from the top of the organisation, carried through in every aspect of its work, attending to both the skills and motivation of staff – are not different from those which any organisation has to adopt to succeed. In Chapter 6 and also in Chapter 7, we emphasise the importance of aligning different organisational processes, including person-centred approaches but also administrative and organisational procedures, so that they work together in an integrated and coherent way to sustain the quality of life of the people the organisation supports.

It also seems clear that what makes life especially difficult for organisations providing support to people with severe or profound intellectual disabilities is that the environment in which they operate is itself ambivalent about what services ought to achieve. None of the organisations with which we have worked, in any country, experiences clear and unremitting support for its work to improve the quality of support it offers to the people with severe or profound intellectual disabilities it serves. Funding agencies seem preoccupied with other concerns – particularly with cost reduction and managing demand for services, often responding to crises rather than in any planned way. Regulators, too, seem heavily focused on what are usually minimum standards, which do not distinguish between services providing good support and those that do not. In both cases, they may be supportive in principle but their primary interest seems to lie elsewhere.

To some extent, the directors and leaders of support-providing organisations can try to insulate their staff from these influences, doing their best to manage external demands and, where possible, to renegotiate them at least not to hinder the provision of good support. The repeated demonstration that active support has good results in enabling people with severe or profound intellectual disabilities to grow in independence, control and inclusion, and the tenacity of organisations and their staff to do their best in spite of obstacles will, it is to be hoped, lead to a shift in the frame of consensus about what is an acceptable level of support.

The future of active support

The key point about active support in practice is that, when surveying the whole field of support for people with severe or profound intellectual disabilities, we are, to use Ian McLean's phrase, still only achieving 'moments of excellence'. Active support is still often misunderstood, fragile and poorly implemented. Strengthening the practice base and then using research to provide evidence of the power of active support to change lives is a priority.

This requires attention to the centrality of 'the enabling relationship' and to practice leadership, rather than to the overwhelming importance given to reorganising management structures so popular in public administration. It also means developing and maintaining the political momentum to make governments, funders and regulators pay attention to quality of life as the most important outcome and to person-centred active support as a critical mechanism for achieving it. This would be entirely consistent with the espoused strategy of evidence-based practice. People with intellectual disabilities, their families, advocates and organisations, together with their supporters in the academic, professional and service communities, all have a role to play in building this coalition of support.

The agenda in support services

For support services (whether the small agency providing help to enable families to use individual budgets to support a family member with severe or profound intellectual disabilities, or the larger organisation providing group homes or other services), there are a number of areas that deserve further exploration. First, there is the task of striking the correct balance between creativity and skill on the one hand and programme fidelity on the other. In our experience, many services employ staff with good ideas about how to support people they serve, but there is no way of organising and integrating these ideas. So what happens is that people receiving support are at the mercy of the latest fad or fashion, or what this team leader thinks is important, or which member of staff is on duty helping them today. Programme fidelity involves sticking to the 'program theory' (Clement and Bigby 2011) – the philosophy of care and 'The Way We Work'; carried to extremes, it can lead to rigid, impersonal care practices that are as institutional as anything from the past. In trying to develop the idea of person-centred active support (Mansell *et al.* 2005), we have tried to strike a balance by harnessing creativity and skill within the context of a working model that is based on sound research evidence.

The changing nature of the service system presents a distinct challenge too. In many countries, services are becoming more decentralised, more fragmented, more dispersed. In these circumstances, coordination becomes more difficult, and there is a risk that each part of the whole service system becomes focused only on its own narrow contribution. How can good person-centred active support be provided consistently across different situations by different organisations? Who will coordinate the process and how much energy will it take to do so?

Further work is also likely to be needed in service organisations to integrate different aspects of person-centred practice into coherent practice frameworks, and then to use these to push back into the systems for training, educating and accrediting staff so that these systems reflect what is needed in practice and do not themselves hinder effective working. One area where this seems particularly important is in recognising the sophistication and skill involved in the enabling relationship: 'life for people with major disabilities in good services will often look quite ordinary, but this ordinariness will be the product of a great deal of careful planning and management' (Department of Health 1993; Department of Health 2007a, paragraph 41).

Finally, support services that help people with other labels, such as people with chronic mental health problems or dementia, may find person-centred active support useful in improving their quality of life. The kinds of help required may not always be the same (for example, person-centred active support emphasises non-verbal communication and graded assistance more than may be necessary in populations that already possess, or have possessed, needed skills) but the general approach may well have a part to play.

The agenda for research

One important area for further research in active support is to explore its effect on quality of life domains other than engagement in meaningful activity and relationships – particularly, to understand better the mixed results reported for community involvement, social relationships, choice and challenging behaviour. The measures used to assess these things are often rather old and may not be detecting important changes, but it also seems likely that weak implementation means that opportunities in these areas are not being realised. This remains a priority for collaboration in research and development between researchers, services and people receiving support.

Most existing research has focused on the living situation: active support would appear to have obvious application in employment, education and leisure services, and research and demonstration projects in these areas would add to the body of knowledge about what is possible and how good practice could be achieved.

Some of the future research agenda is not specific to active support per se. We need to know more about the effects of organisational culture – both the formal culture of the service-providing organisation and the informal culture of the staff group – on the implementation of person-centred practices. Bluntly, we need to know why it is so easy to get things wrong and keep them that way, and so difficult to establish and sustain good practice over the longer period.

There are also interesting issues to be explored about training. Many of the staff now working with people with severe or profound intellectual disabilities have a background that includes a strong training in normalisation values and a strong grounding in applied behaviour analysis. Disability training now does not pay nearly as much attention to these areas. It is more generic and adopts a social model which risks ignoring the reality of people's impairments. Person-centred active support might require a good basic understanding both of the values in normalisation (as well as in the human-rights approach of the UN Convention) and of fundamental behavioural skills (ecological manipulation, prompting, shaping, fading, reinforcement and so on). If the stock of people who have this knowledge is not being replaced, it may be much more difficult to provide active support in the future.

In many Western service systems there is increased fragmentation, reflecting the introduction of individual budgets and other attempts to give disabled people more control over the services they receive (and also perhaps to save money). In some countries this has gone alongside the wider use of non-government and, especially, profit-making services. It is not clear how, in this context, a coherent sense of direction, shared values and practical arrangements for working together can be achieved.

Research specifically in active support needs to address the evaluation of developments undertaken by service-providing organisations and also to evaluate the effect of these wider policy changes on what really happens to people receiving services. Where poor quality of life is found, it is the responsibility of researchers to be able to identify whether this is due to the impossibility of ameliorating people's disabilities, given the present state of knowledge, or whether it is due to weak implementation and, if so, why that might be. Our experience is that poor results are always due to weak implementation; that all individuals with severe or profound intellectual disabilities can have their quality of life transformed, at least in some ways and to some extent, whatever their problems.

Summary of the levels of engagement reported in available studies and additional analysis of available data, with Adaptive Behaviour Scale Part 1 (ABS) score where available

Paper	Brief description of study	Number of participants for which data presented	ABS score (mean and range)	% non-social engagement (range)	% social engagement (range)	% total engagement (range)
Hughes and Mansell (1990)[1] and Mansell, Hughes and McGill (1994)[2]	Report of baseline data in Camberwell study – evaluation for London borough providing for 100 people in staffed community houses and a 40-place campus-style service (20 homes in total). NB Averages calculated from Appendix 6 of report.	45 people in the 4 staffed houses	Not available	26.7 (7.7–58.1)	5.1 (0.6–12.4)	
Hughes and Mansell (1992)[3]	Camberwell study baseline data for the wider group of 20 services.	Repeated for 20 services across the borough.		15		
Hewson (1991)[4] and Hewson and Walker (1992)[5]	Evaluation of reprovision to 10 community-based houses run by NHS. MTS 30 second interval, 2 3-hour periods in each home (10am–1pm and 4–7 pm).	59 adults	Not given			50 (25–65.1)
Emerson et al. (1992)[6]	Evaluation of quality of life in 2 community-based houses	8 people with severe ID and severe CB	Not available		3	13.6 (8–24)

Mansell and Barrett (1993)[7]	Evaluation/audit of services in London Borough of Southwark. Used MTS rotating around individuals for 10 minutes at a time between 4pm and 7pm. Some summary data calculated from graphs in report.	18 people with severe and profound ID and challenging behaviour	Not available	18% in leisure (mainly TV), 13% in personal care, 0.3% in practical tasks involving gas or electrical equipment, 6% in simple practical tasks, 0.5% in gardening	7	43 (22.7–59.2 across 7 houses)
Orlowska and Mansell (1996)[8]	Follows up audit from Mansell and Barrett (1993). Following intervention although not active support per se. Completed procedural guidance for staff, increase staff skills, refocus first- and second-line management on practice leadership, refocus information collection on quality to help translate values into action. Open up culture of the services. Retrained first-line and middle managers. Data from whole-day observations presented on page 11 (Figure 3) are summarised here	9 services	Not presented although analysis using ABS			39 (10–59)
Moore and Mansell (1998)[9]	Audit following further recommendations for improving the services assessed in Mansell and Barrett (1993).	Data collected in 7 of the original services	Not available			35
Felce, Lowe and Blackman (1995)[10]	Comparison of community-based and hospital provision. 16 people, 8 in hospital who then moved to community and 8 in community setting.	8 (adults with severe ID and severe CB) living in community		21 (7–39)	9 (0–30)	28 (7–62)

		Sample	5 of above sample in small group homes	27		
Felce and Perry (1995)[11]	Looked at situation of people who moved from institutions into 15 staffed homes (1–7 places).	57 adults (54 at the end)	164 (61–254) (calculated from home level data provided in paper)	49 (13–88)		54
Jones et al. (1999)[12]	Evaluation of implementation of active support in 5 staffed community services. (NB ranges are for services not people.)	19 adults aged 30–67 (mean age 48)	115 (12–236)	25.2 (17.6–32.9)	11.8 (7.5–15.4)	33.1 (22.7–39.5)
Emerson et al. (1999a)[13]	Study looking at relationships between engagement, staff contact and stereotypy.	40 adults with intellectual disabilities and living in 4 different settings. Many with sensory impairments.	Not used			16.9 (3.8–47.9)
Emerson et al. (1999b)[14]	Observational study of dispersed housing (group homes and SL), and NHS residential campuses, 40 participants in 12 services. 20 in 5 NHS campuses and 20 in 5 independent dispersed settings and 1 NHS dispersed setting.	20 people living in dispersed housing	Dispersed housing sample 39.6 (SD 16)	11	1.8	2–42 (only range provided to illustrate variation)
Jones et al. (2001a)[15]	Evaluation of the implementation of active support training in 38 community group homes, with 303 staff and 106 people with ID.	106 people	144 (20–293)			46.7

Study	Description					
Jones et al. (2001b)[16]	Explored the outcomes for people in different training groups – 22 services researchers did training; 16 managers did training but with supervision from researchers; 36 managers were left to do training on their own.	188 people; 58 in Phase 1, 48 in Phase 2 and 82 in Phase 3	156 (20–293) NB Phase 1 people had lower ABS scores – mean 129 compared with 163 and 170	Phase 1: 31.6 Phase 2: 40.4 Phase 3: 52.5	Phase 1: 15 Phase 2: 18.8 Phase 3: 22.9	Phase 1: 41.8 Phase 2: 52.5 Phase 3: 58
Bradshaw et al. (2004)[17]	Implementation of active support in 3 homes from one voluntary sector provider. 33 staff trained in active support.	10 people with severe to profound ID in houses where AS implemented; 12 people in comparison houses	AS group: 94 (39–179, calculated from Table 3) Comparison group: 88 (29–173)			AS group: 16.6 Comparison group T1: 29.2 Comparison group T2: 20.8
Additional analysis of sample described in Ashman and Beadle-Brown (2006)[18]	Evaluation of services in one national charity 5 years after implementation of active support. Data presented here is for a sub sample of the 469 people for whom findings were reported in the report. This analysis for people who were not receiving good consistent active support.	168	103 (0–223)	18 (0–85)	11 (0–80)	28 (0–100)
	Analysis repeated for people with ABS part 1 scores < 181 who were not rated as receiving good active support.	125	89 (29–171)	14 (0–80)	9 (0–80)	23 (0–97)

Stancliffe et al. (2007)[19]	Follow-up data of implementation of active support for 22 people in 5 services – 3 NGO, 2 DHS.	22 people age 41 (27–62 years)	Used ICAP – range of disabilities			42.46 (SD 22.39)
Mansell et al. (2008)[20]	Group comparison of 36 homes where managers had been trained as trainers and 36 homes where managers had not been trained. More able sample. Groups matched on ABS and other characteristics. 359 people in total.	169 people in the PCAS group; 190 in comparison group.	PCAS group: SABS % 58.31 (SD 23.64). ABS calculated 182. Comparison group: SABS 55.82 (SD 24). ABS calculated 173.			70 (SD 24)
Netten et al. (2010)[21]	Large national survey of 173 care homes for people with intellectual disability and older adults. One point in time study of outcomes of people in care homes.	375 people with ID; observational data available for 336 people	ABS 125 (24–279; SD 59.6) (calculated for the purpose of this comparison)	39 (0–100)	12 (0–78)	50 (0–100)

Totsika et al. (2010)[22]	Looked at quality of life of people with intellectual disabilities who were older, with and without autism. Initial sample was 819 adults collated from 5 studies. 34% had autism and mean ABS was 168, mean AMC 29.7. 31 people lived independently, 142 in family situation and 646 in group homes. Selected those over 50.	282 people who were over 50, with and without autism	With autism: 119.1 (SD 46.1) Without autism: 118.9 (SD 55.7)		With autism: 38.8 (SD 22.2) Without autism: 58.7 (SD 25.1)
	Compared a matched group of those with and without autism over 50.	82, 41 with autism and 41 without, matched on ABS	With autism: 140.8 Without autism: 139.4		With autism: 45 (SD 21.3) Without autism: 40.4 (SD 24.6)
	Compared younger people with autism and older people with autism.	194 younger people with autism, 87 older people with autism	Younger people with autism: 119 (SD 61) Older people with autism: 119.1 (SD 46.1)		Younger people with autism: 42.4 (SD 26.9) Older people with autism: 38.8 (SD 22.2)
Perry et al. (2011)[23]	Looked at changes in outcomes and situation for people with challenging behaviour who moved out of hospital into community-based settings. Data given for follow-up.	21 adults aged 47 years (36–67). Data presented for 19 people at follow-up (once in community)	162	Interaction with staff: 17.7 (SD 15) Interaction with service users: 2.25	48.4 (SD 29.9)

Beadle-Brown et al. (2011)[24]	Study looking at changes before and after whole-environment training on active support.	29 people with severe and profound intellectual disability	77.4 (27–154)	15 (0–59)	6 (0–36)	20 (0–82)
Mansell et al. (2011)[25]	Data collected across 6 organisations at different stages of implementing PCAS. This was baseline data before intervention of work with house supervisors and senior managers.	Whole sample 131 people with intellectual disabilities and some challenging behaviour.	153 (39–253)	42 (0–100)	9 (0–66)	52 (0–100)
		70 people with more severe disabilities (ABS<181)	118 (39–180)	37 (0–100)	7 (0–58)	44 (0–100)
		61 (excluding those receiving higher levels of active support)	112 (39–180)	34 (0–100)	5 (0–30)	40 (0–100)
Beadle-Brown et al. (2011)[26]	Audit of services provided by a national charity which had been implementing active support for approximately 10 years. Data presented here is for sub sample of people with ABS less than 181 where active support was not being implemented	102	71 (0–166)	71 (0–166)	7 (0–53)	22 (0–100)

References

1   Hughes, H. and Mansell, J. (1990) *Consultation to Camberwell Health Authority Learning Difficulties Care Group: Evaluation Report.* Canterbury: Centre for the Applied Psychology of Social Care, University of Kent.

2   Mansell, J., Hughes, H. and McGill, P. (1994) 'Maintaining Local Residential Placements.' In E. Emerson, P. McGill and J. Mansell (eds) *Severe Learning Disabilities and Challenging Behaviour: Designing High-Quality Services.* London: Chapman and Hall, pp.260–81.

3   Hughes, H. and Mansell, J. (1992) *Consultation to Camberwell Health Authority Learning Difficulties Care Group: Intervention Report.* Canterbury: Centre for the Applied Psychology of Social Care, University of Kent.

4   Hewson, S. (1991) 'The evaluation of quality in a mental handicap service.' *International Journal of Health Care Quality Assurance 4,* 3, 18–22.

5   Hewson, S. and Walker, J. (1992) 'The use of evaluation in the development of a staffed residential service for adults with mental handicap.' *Mental Handicap Research 5,* 2, 188–203.

6   Emerson, E., Beasley, F., Offord, G. and Mansell, J. (1992) 'Specialised housing for people with seriously challenging behaviours.' *Journal of Mental Deficiency Research 36,* 291–307.

7   Mansell, J. and Barrett, S. (1993) *An Audit of Southwark Social Services for People with Learning Disabilities: Final Report.* Canterbury: Centre for the Applied Psychology of Social Care (now the Tizard Centre).

8   Orlowska, D. and Mansell, J. (1996) *Second Audit of Southwark Residential Services for People with Learning Disabilities.* Canterbury: Tizard Centre.

9   Moore, J. and Mansell, J. (1998) *Residential Services for People with Learning Disabilities Provided by the London Borough of Southwark: Five-Year Follow-Up.* Canterbury: Tizard Centre.

10 Felce, D., Lowe, K. and Blackman, D. (1995) 'Resident behaviour and staff interaction with people with intellectual disabilities and seriously challenging behaviour in residential services.' *Mental Handicap Research 8,* 272–95.

11 Felce, D. and Perry, J. (1995) 'The extent of support for ordinary living provided in staffed housing: The relationship between staffing levels, resident characteristics, staff:resident interactions and resident activity patterns.' *Social Science and Medicine 40,* 6, 799–810.

12 Jones, E., Perry, J., Lowe, K., Felce, D. *et al.* (1999) 'Opportunity and the promotion of activity among adults with severe intellectual disability living in community residences: The impact of training staff in active support.' *Journal of Intellectual Disability Research 43,* 3, 164–78.

13 Emerson, E., Hatton, C., Robertson, J., Henderson, D. and Cooper, J. (1999a) 'A descriptive analysis of the relationships between social context, engagement and stereotypy in residential services for people with severe and complex disabilities.' *Journal of Applied Research in Intellectual Disabilities 12,* 1, 11–29.

14 Emerson, E., Robertson, J., Gregory, N., Kessissoglou, S. *et al.* (1999b) *Quality and Costs of Residential Supports for People with Learning Disabilities: An Observational Study of Supports Provided to People with Severe and Complex Learning Disabilities in Residential Campuses and Dispersed Housing Schemes.* Manchester: Hester Adrian Research Centre.

15 Jones, E., Felce, D., Lowe, K., Bowley, C. *et al.* (2001a) 'Evaluation of the dissemination of active support training in staffed community residences.' *American Journal on Mental Retardation 106,* 4, 344–58.

16 Jones, E., Felce, D., Lowe, K., Bowley, C. *et al.* (2001b) 'Evaluation of the dissemination of active support training and training trainers.' *Journal of Applied Research in Intellectual Disabilities 14*, 2, 79–99.

17 Bradshaw, J., McGill, P., Stretton, R., Kelly-Pike, A. *et al.* (2004) 'Implementation and evaluation of active support.' *Journal of Applied Research in Intellectual Disabilities 17*, 3, 139–48.

18 Ashman, B. and Beadle-Brown, J. (2006) *A Valued Life: Developing Person-Centred Approaches So People Can Be More Included.* London: United Response.

19 Stancliffe, R.J., Harman, A., Toogood, S. and McVilly, K.R. (2007) 'Australian implementation and evaluation of active support.' *Journal of Applied Research in Intellectual Disabilities 20*, 3, 211–27.

20 Mansell, J., Beadle-Brown, J., Whelton, R., Beckett, C. and Hutchinson, A. (2008) 'Effect of service structure and organisation on staff care practices in small community homes for people with intellectual disabilities.' *Journal of Applied Research in Intellectual Disabilities 21*, 3, 398–413.

21 Netten, A., Beadle-Brown, J., Trukeschitz, B., Towers, A. *et al.* (2010) *Measuring the Outcomes of Care Homes: Final Report* (Discussion Paper 2696/2). Canterbury: Personal Social Services Research Unit, University of Kent.

22 Totsika, V., Felce, D., Kerr, M. and Hastings, R.P. (2010). 'Behavior problems, psychiatric symptoms, and quality of life for older adults with intellectual disability with and without autism.' *Journal of Autism and Developmental Disorders 40*, 10, 1171–8.

23 Perry, J., Felce, D., Allen, D. and Meek, A. (2011) 'Resettlement outcomes for people with severe challenging behaviour moving from institutional to community living.' *Journal of Applied Research in Intellectual Disabilities 24*, 1–17.

24 Beadle-Brown, J., Hutchinson, A. and Whelton, B. (2012) 'Person-centred active support: Increasing choice, promoting independence and reducing challenging behaviour.' *Journal of Applied Research in Intellectual Disabilities.*

25 Mansell, J., Beadle-Brown, J., Bigby, C., Mountford, L. and Clement, T. (2011) *Active Support Implementation in Victoria: Report to Chief Executives.* Melbourne, Australia: La Trobe University.

26 Beadle-Brown, J., Ashman, A., Ockendon, J., Isles, R., Whelton, B. and Mansell, J. (2011) *Evaluation of Active Support Over Time.* Canterbury: Tizard Centre.

Summary of data on engagement and support from staff following implementation of active support

Paper	Description	n	ABS score	% NSA	% SA	% Any engage.	% Assist.	% Other cont.	% Any cont.	ASM (% score)
Mansell et al. (1984)[1]	Study looking at levels of engagement in one of Andover houses – people with severe and profound disabilities.	6	Not available			Ranged from 20 to 80%; 3 people were engaged more than 50% of the time on every occasion. Other 3 (including 2 short-term residents) engaged between 20 and 30% of the time.				
Felce et al. (1986)[2]	Describing the first 2 Andover houses – active support a critical part of the practices in the 2 houses	12 (6 in each house)	House 1: 117 (62–168) House 2: 105 (54–143)	House 1: 51 House 2: 56	House 1: 17 House 2: 4		House 1: 22 (80% of contact) House 2: 14		House 1: 27 House 2: 20	

Study	Description	Sample						
Hughes and Mansell (1992)[3]	Camberwell study baseline data for the wider group of 20 services. (NB active support not maintained across time.)	Repeated for 20 services across the borough		15% across 20 services at baseline 17% in 1990 12% in 1992				11% across 20 services at baseline 12% in 1990 9% in 1991
Jones et al. (1999)[4]	Evaluation of implementation of active support in 5 staffed community services. (NB ranges are for services not people.)	19 adults aged 30–67 (mean age 48)	115 (12–236)	Pre: 25.2 (17.6–32.9) Post: 54.5 (52.6–62)	Pre: 11.8 (7.5–15.4) Post: 15.4 (4.6–21.2)	Pre: 33.1 (22.7–39.5) Post: 57.2 (49.7–63.6)	Pre: 5.9 (2.8–8.2) Post: 16 (11.4–26.2)	Pre: 17.5 (13.8–22) Post: 28.2 (43.4)
Jones et al. (2001a)[5]	Evaluation of the implementation of active support training in 38 community group homes, with 303 staff and 106 people with ID.	106 people aged 22–76 (mean 43)	144 (20–293)			Pre: 46.7 Post: 54.6	Pre: 7.5 Post: 14.6	

Jones et al. (2001b)[6]	Explored the outcomes for people in different training groups. Phase 1: 22 services researchers did training; Phase 2: 16 service managers did training but with super-vision from researchers; Phase 3: 36 managers were left to do training on their own	188 people aged 21–79 (mean 45); 58 in Phase 1, 48 in Phase 2 and 82 in Phase 3	156 (20–293) NB Phase 1 peo-ple had lower ABS scores – mean 129 compared with 163 and 170.	Baseline Phase 1: 31.6 Phase 2: 40.4 Phase 3: 52.5 Post: Phase 1: 43.7 Phase 2: 45.9 Phase 3: 56.1	Baseline Phase 1: 15 Phase 2: 18.8 Phase 3: 22.9 Post: Phase 1: 14.5 Phase 2: 17.4 Phase 3: 20.9	Baseline Phase 1: 41.8 Phase 2: 52.5 Phase 3: 58 Post: Phase 1: 53.4 Phase 2: 56.1 Phase 3: 57	Baseline Phase 1: verbal 6.8, non-verbal 3.8 Phase 2: verbal 5.7, non-verbal 2.7 Phase 3: verbal 6, non-verbal 3 Post: Phase 1: verbal 14.1, non-verbal 12.3 Phase 2: verbal 9.2, non-verbal 5.8 Phase 3: verbal 4, non-verbal 2	Baseline Phase 1: 14 Phase 2: 15.8 Phase 3: 20.8 Post: Phase 1: 14.1 Phase 2: 13.9 Phase 3: 20.4

Study	Description							
Mansell et al. (2002)[7]	Engagement is the % of total possible score on a rating scale. Compares services implementing active support with those not doing so.	23	Not available		No AS implementation: 7 AS implemented: 33%			No/weak AS implementation: 50 AS implemented: 66
Bradshaw et al. (2004)[8]	Implementation of active support in 3 homes from one voluntary sector provider. 33 staff trained in active support.	10 people with severe to profound ID in houses where AS implemented 12 people in comparison houses	AS group 94 (39–179) n = 9, calculated from Table 3 Comparison group 88 (29–173)		AS group T1 16.6% Comparison son group T1 29.2% AS group T2 26% Comparison son group T2 20.8%		AS group T1 16.7% Comparison son group T1 16.2% Comparison son group T2 13.1% AS group T2 21.2%	

Ashman and Beadle-Brown (2006)[9]								
Evaluation of services in one national charity 5 years after implementation of active support – treated as follow-up data as organisation had implemented active support.	469 people observed, mainly a range of needs but on average in the severe disability range	Not provided in report	30		43			63%
Secondary analysis of original data used in Ashman and Beadle-Brown (2006)	303 with observational data	127.3 (29–265)	30 (10–98)	14 (0–100)	43 (0–100)	11 (0–64)	19 (0–80)	61 (10–97)
Results for whole sample of people with ABS score below 181.	219	102 (29–178)	24 (0–95)	12 (0–80)	35 (0–100)	11 (0–64)	18 (0–100)	56 (0–97)

					Pre: 42.46 (SD 22.39) Post: 53.81 (SD 26.19)	Pre: 7.3 (SD 6.79) Post: 13.56 (SD 12.21)		
Stancliffe et al. (2007)[10]	Follow-up data of implementation of active support for 22 people in 5 services – 3 NGO, 2 DHS. 131-day follow-up.	22 people age 41 (27–62 years)	Used ICAP – mixed ability group but more on the more able end of the scale					
Mansell et al. (2008)[11]	Group comparison of 36 homes where managers had been trained as trainers and 36 homes where managers had not been trained. More able sample. Groups matched on ABS and other characteristics. 359 people in total. Follow-up 5 months after training.	169 people in the PCAS group; 190 in comparison group	PCAS SABS % 58.31 (SD 23.64) ABS calculated 182. Comparison SABS: 55.82 (SD 24) ABS calculated 173.		Comparison group: 70 (SD 24) PCAS group: 77 (SD 21)	Comparison group: 8% (SD 11) PCAS group: 12 (SD 15)	Comparison group 15 (SD 16) PCAS group: 18 (16)	Comparison son group: 54.13 (24.25) PCAS group: 65.28 (SD 23.46)

Totsika *et al.* (2010)[12]	Study looking at the effect of interactive training 13 months after classroom-based training.	21 adults with ID	Not provided	Pre 34% (SD 21.8) Follow-up 36% (SD 21.7)	Pre 8% (SD 10.2) Follow-up 8% (SD 8.1)	Pre 41% (SD 23.8) Follow-up 42% (SD 22.7)	Pre 8% (SD 5.1) Follow-up 9% (SD 7.2)		Pre 16% (SD 7.9) Follow-up 19% (SD 10.08)	Pre (mean) 24 (SD 6.5) Follow-up (mean) 23.35 (SD 9.04)
Beadle-Brown *et al.* (2012)[13]	Study looking at changes before and after whole-environment training on active support.	29 people with severe and profound ID	77.4 (27–154)	Pre: 15 (0–59) Post: 29 (0–86)	Pre: 6 (0–36) Post: 14 (0–39)	Pre: 20 (0–82) Post: 41 (0–91)	Pre: 2 (0–24) Post: 10 (0–47)	Pre: 12 (0–46) Post: 16 (0–43)		Pre: 34 (17–54) Post: 64 (25–93)
Beadle-Brown *et al.* (2011)[14]	Audit of services provided by a national charity which had been implementing active support for approximately 10 years. Data counted as post implementation of AS.	284 people with full observation data	120.37 (0–267)	25 (0–100)	14 (0–80)	45 (0–100)	10 (0–80)	22 (0–80)		68 (8–100)

Sub sample of those with ABS less than 181 from Beadle-Brown et al. (in preparation)	216	91 (0–177)	19 (0–96)	12 (0–80)	35 (0–100)	10 (0–80)	21 (0–80)		62 (8–100)

NSA = non-social activity
SA = social activity
Any engage. = any engagement
Assist. = assistance
Cont. = contact (from staff)
ASM = active support measure

References

1   Mansell, J., Jenkins, J., Felce, D. and de Kock, U. (1984) 'Measuring the activity of severely and profoundly mentally handicapped adults in ordinary housing.' *Behaviour Research and Therapy 22*, 1, 23–9.

2   Felce, D., de Kock, U. and Repp, A.C. (1986) 'An eco-behavioural comparison of small community-based houses and traditional large hospitals for severely and profoundly mentally handicapped adults.' *Applied Research in Mental Retardation 7*, 393–408.

3   Hughes, H. and Mansell, J. (1992) *Consultation to Camberwell Health Authority Learning Difficulties Care Group: Intervention Report.* Canterbury: Centre for the Applied Psychology of Social Care, University of Kent.

4   Jones, E. Perry, J., Lowe, K., Felce, D. *et al.* (1999) 'Opportunity and the promotion of activity among adults with severe intellectual disability living in community residences: The impact of training staff in active support.' *Journal of Intellectual Disability Research 43*, 3, 164–78.

5   Jones, E., Felce, D., Lowe, K., Bowley, C. *et al.* (2001a) 'Evaluation of the dissemination of active support training in staffed community residences.' *American Journal on Mental Retardation 106*, 4, 344–58.

6   Jones, E., Felce, D., Lowe, K., Bowley, C. *et al.* (2001b) 'Evaluation of the dissemination of active support training and training trainers.' *Journal of Applied Research in Intellectual Disabilities 14*, 2, 79–99.

7   Mansell, J., Elliott, T., Beadle-Brown, J., Ashman, B. and Macdonald, S. (2002) 'Engagement in meaningful activity and "active support" of people with intellectual disabilities in residential care.' *Research in Developmental Disabilities 23*, 5, 342–52.

8   Bradshaw, J., McGill, P., Stretton, R., Kelly-Pike, A. *et al.* (2004) 'Implementation and evaluation of active support.' *Journal of Applied Research in Intellectual Disabilities 17*, 3, 139–48.

9   Ashman, B. and Beadle-Brown, J. (2006) *A Valued Life: Developing Person-Centred Approaches So People Can Be More Included.* London: United Response.

10 Stancliffe, R.J., Harman, A., Toogood, S. and McVilly, K.R. (2007) 'Australian implementation and evaluation of active support.' *Journal of Applied Research in Intellectual Disabilities 20*, 3, 211–27.

11 Mansell, J., Beadle-Brown, J., Whelton, R., Beckett, C. and Hutchinson, A. (2008) 'Effect of service structure and organisation on staff care practices in small community homes for people with intellectual disabilities.' *Journal of Applied Research in Intellectual Disabilities 21*, 3, 398–413.

12 Totsika, V., Toogood, S., Hastings, R. and McCarthy, J. (2010) 'The effect of active support interactive training on the daily lives of adults with an intellectual disability.' *Journal of Applied Research in Intellectual Disabilities 23*, 112–21.

13 Beadle-Brown, J., Hutchinson, A. and Whelton, B. (2012) 'Person-centred active support: Increasing choice, promoting independence and reducing challenging behaviour.' *Journal of Applied Research in Intellectual Disabilities.*

14 Beadle-Brown, J., Mansell, J., Ashman, A., Ockendon, J, Iles, R. and Whelton, B. (2011) *Evaluation of active support over time.* Canterbury: Tizard Centre.

References

Accreditation Council on Services for Mentally Retarded and Other Developmentally Disabled Persons (1983) *Standards for Services for Developmentally Disabled Individuals.* Chicago, IL: Joint Commission on Accreditation of Hospitals.

Allen, P., Pahl, J. and Quine, L. (1990) *Care Staff in Transition.* London: Her Majesty's Stationery Office.

Aman, M.G., Singh, N.N., Stewart, A.W. and Field, C.J. (1985) 'The aberrant behavior checklist: A behavior rating scale for the assessment of treatment effects.' *American Journal of Mental Deficiency 89,* 5, 485–91.

American Association on Intellectual and Developmental Disabilities and ARC of the United States (2010) *Behavioral Supports: Joint Position Statement.* Washington, DC: American Association on Intellectual and Developmental Disabilities and ARC of the United States.

Anderson, S.R. (1987) 'The Management of Staff Behaviour in Residential Treatment Facilities: A Review of Training Techniques.' In J. Hogg and P. Mittler (eds) *Staff Training in Mental Handicap.* Beckenham: Croom Helm, pp.66–124.

Arscott, K., Dagnan, D. and Kroese, B.S. (1999) 'Assessing the ability of people with a learning disability to give informed consent to treatment.' *Psychological Medicine 29,* 6, 1367–75.

Ashman, B. and Beadle-Brown, J. (2006) *A Valued Life: Developing Person-Centred Approaches So People Can Be More Included.* London: United Response.

Ashman, B., Ockendon, J., Beadle-Brown, J. and Mansell, J. (2010) *Person-Centred Active Support: A Handbook.* Brighton: Pavilion.

Balla, D.A. (1976) 'Relationship of institution size to quality of care: A review of literature.' *American Journal of Mental Deficiency 81,* 2, 117–24.

Barton, R. (1959) *Institutional Neurosis.* Bristol: Wright.

Baumeister, A.A. and Zaharia, E.S. (1987) 'Withdrawal and Commitment of Basic-Care Staff in Residential Programs.' In S. Landesman and P. Vietze (eds) *Living Environments and Mental Retardation.* Washington, DC: American Association on Mental Retardation, pp.229–67.

Beadle-Brown, J., Ashman, A., Ockendon, J., Isles, R., Whelton, B. and Mansell, J. (2011) *Evaluation of Active Support Over Time.* Canterbury: Tizard Centre.

Beadle-Brown, J., Hutchinson, A. and Mansell, J. (2005) *Care Standards in Homes for People with Intellectual Disabilities.* Canterbury: Tizard Centre.

Beadle-Brown, J., Hutchinson, A. and Whelton, B. (2012) 'Person-centred active support: Increasing choice, promoting independence and reducing challenging behaviour.' *Journal of Applied Research in Intellectual Disabilities.*

Beadle-Brown, J., Mansell, J., Ashman, A., Ockendon, J. *et al.* (submitted) 'The role of practice leadership in improving quality in intellectual disability services for people with intellectual disabilities: an exploratoy sudy.' *Journal of Intellectual Disability Research.*

Beadle-Brown, J., Mansell, J., Ashman, B., Ockenden, J. and Whelton, B. (2008) 'The role of practice leadership in improving and maintaining quality in intellectual disability services.' Paper presented at 13th IASSID World Congress, 25–30 August 2008, Cape Town, South Africa. *Journal of Intellectual Disability Research 52,* 8–9, 755.

Beadle-Brown, J. and Mills, R. (2010) *Understanding and Supporting Children and Adults on the Autism Spectrum.* Brighton: Pavilion.

Beadle-Brown, J., Vallis, T. and Mansell, J. (2006) 'An exploratory study of the priorities, activities and competencies of managers in residential services for people with intellectual disabilities.' Paper presented at 2nd European Congress of the International Association for the Scientific Study of Intellectual Disabilities, 2–5 August 2006, Maastricht, Netherlands. *Journal of Applied Research in Intellectual Disabilities 19,* 3, 229.

Belbin, R.M. (1997) *Management Teams: Why They Succeed or Fail.* Oxford: Butterworth-Heinemann.

Bellamy, G.T., Newton, J.S., LeBaron, N.M. and Horner, R.H. (1986) *Toward Lifestyle Accountability in Residential Services for Persons with Mental Retardation.* Eugene: Specialized Training Program.

Bellamy, G.T., Newton, J.S., LeBaron, N.M. and Horner, R.H. (1990) 'Quality of Life and Lifestyle Outcome: A Challenge for Residential Programs.' In R.L. Schalock and M.J. Begab (eds) *Quality of Life: Perspectives and Issues.* Washington, DC: American Association on Mental Retardation, pp.127–37.

Bigby, C., Clement, T., Mansell, J. and Beadle-Brown, J. (2009) 'It's pretty hard with our ones, they can't talk, the more able-bodied can participate': Staff attitudes about the applicability of disability policies to people with severe and profound intellectual disabilities.' *Journal of Intellectual Disability Research 53*, 4, 363–76.

Bigby, C., Cooper, B.K. and Reid, K. (2010) *Making Life Good in the Community: Measures of Resident Outcomes and Staff Perceptions of the Move from an Institution.* Melbourne, Australia: La Trobe University.

Bigby, C., Knox, M., Beadle-Brown, J., Clement, T. and Mansell, J. (in press) 'Uncovering dimensions of informal culture in underperforming group homes for people with severe intellectual disabilities.' *Intellectual and Developmental Disabilities.*

Biklen, D. (1993) *Communication Unbound: How Facilitated Communication is Challenging Traditional Views of Autism and Ability/Disability.* New York, NY: Teachers College Press.

Blunden, R. (1980) *Individual Plans for Mentally Handicapped People: A Procedural Guide.* Cardiff: Mental Handicap in Wales Applied Research Unit.

Bradshaw, J. (2001) 'Complexity of staff communication and reported level of understanding skills in adults with intellectual disability.' *Journal of Intellectual Disability Research 45*, 3, 233–43.

Bradshaw, J., McGill, P., Stretton, R., Kelly-Pike, A. *et al.* (2004) 'Implementation and evaluation of active support.' *Journal of Applied Research in Intellectual Disabilities 17*, 3, 139–48.

Brandford, S. (2008) 'Evaluation of Total Communication in residential services: Introducing culture shift.' *Journal of Intellectual Disability Research 52*, 676.

British Broadcasting Corporation (2011) *Undercover Care: The Abuse Exposed.* London: British Broadcasting Corporation.

Bromley, J. and Emerson, E. (1995) 'Beliefs and emotional reactions of care staff working with people with challenging behaviour.' *Journal of Intellectual Disability Research 39*, 4, 341–52.

Brost, M., Johnson, T.Z., Wagner, L. and Deprey, R.K. (1982) *Getting to Know You: One Approach to Service Assessment and Planning for Individuals with Disabilities.* Madison, WI: Wisconsin Coalition for Advocacy.

Brown, H. and Bailey, R. (1987a) *Designing Services to Meet Individual Needs.* Brighton: Pavilion.

Brown, H. and Bailey, R. (1987b) *Working with Families.* Brighton: Pavilion.

Brown, H., Bell, C. and Brown, V. (1988) *Teaching New Skills.* Brighton: Pavilion.

Brown, H. and Brown, V. (1988) *Understanding and Responding to Difficult Behaviour.* Brighton: Pavilion.

Brown, H. and Brown, V. (1989) *Building Social Networks.* Brighton: Pavilion.

Brown, H. and Smith, H. (1992) 'Assertion, Not Assimilation: A Feminist Perspective on the Normalisation Principle.' In H. Brown and H. Smith (eds) *Normalisation: A Reader for the Nineties.* London: Routledge, pp.149–71.

Brown, H., Toogood, A. and Brown, V. (1987) *Participation in Everyday Activities.* Brighton: Pavilion.

Brown, L., Branston-McClean, M., Baumgart, D., Vincent, I., Falvey, M. and Schroeder, J. (1979) 'Using the characteristics of current and subsequent least restrictive environments in the development of curricular content for severely handicapped students.' *AAESPH Review 4*, 4, 407–24.

Bunning, K. (2008) 'Making connections: Evaluation of a total communication strategy in services for adults with ID.' *Journal of Intellectual Disability Research 52*, 677.

Caldwell, P (2006) Finding You Finding Me: Using Intensive Interaction to Get in Touch with People Whose Severe Learning Disabilities Are Combined with Autistic Spectrum Disorder London: Jessica Kingsley.

Caldwell, P., & Horwood, J. (2007). *From isolation to intimacy: making friends without words.* London: Jessica Kingsley.

Caldwell, P., & Horwood, J. (2008). *Using intensive interaction and sensory integration: a handbook for those who support people with severe autistic spectrum disorder.* London: Jessica Kingsley.

Caldwell, P. (2011) *Intensive Interaction: Using Body Language to Communicate.* London: St George's Hospital Medical School.

Cambridge, P. (1999) 'The first hit: A case study of the physical abuse of people with learning disabilities and challenging behaviours in a residential service.' *Disability & Society 14,* 3, 285–308.

Cambridge, P., Carpenter, J., Beecham, J., Hallam, A. *et al.* (2001) *Twelve Years On: The Outcomes and Costs of Community Care for People with Learning Disabilities and Mental Health Problems.* Canterbury: Tizard Centre, University of Kent at Canterbury.

Cannella, H.I., O'Reilly, M.F. and Lancioni, G.E. (2005) 'Choice and preference assessment research with people with severe to profound developmental disabilities: A review of the literature.' *Research in Developmental Disabilities 26,* 1, 1–15.

Carr, E.G. (1977) 'The motivation of self-injurious behavior: A review of some hypotheses.' *Psychological Bulletin 84,* 4, 800–11.

Carr, E.G. (1994) *Communication-Based Intervention for Problem Behavior: A User's Guide for Producing Positive Change.* Baltimore, MD: Paul H. Brookes.

Carr, E.G., Dunlap, G., Horner, R.H., Koegel, R.L. *et al.* (2002) 'Positive behavior support: Evolution of an applied science.' *Journal of Positive Behavior Interventions 4,* 1, 4–16.

Carr, E.G. and Durand, V.M. (1985) 'Reducing behavior problems through functional communication training.' *Journal of Applied Behavior Analysis 18,* 111–26.

Carr, E.G., Horner, R.H., Turnbull, A.P., Marquis, J.G. *et al.* (1999) *Positive Behavior Support for People with Developmental Disabilities: A Research Synthesis.* Washington, DC: American Association on Mental Retardation.

Carr, J.H. and Collins, S. (1992) *Working Towards Independence: A Practical Guide to Teaching People with Learning Disabilities.* London: Jessica Kingsley Publishers.

Challis, D. and Davies, B. (1986) *Case Management in Community Care.* Aldershot: Gower.

Cherniss, C. (1980) *Staff Burnout: Job Stress in the Human Services.* Beverley Hills, CA: Sage Publications.

Clarke, S., Dunlap, G., Foster-Johnson, L., Childs, K.E. *et al.* (1995) 'Improving the conduct of students with behavioral disorders by incorporating student interests into curricular activities.' *Behavioral Disorders 20,* 4, 221–37.

Clement, T. and Bigby, C. (2010) *Group Homes for People with Intellectual Disabilities: Encouraging Inclusion and Participation.* London: Jessica Kingsley Publishers.

Clement, T. and Bigby, C. (2011) 'The development and utility of a program theory: Lessons from an evaluation of a reputed exemplary residential support service for adults with intellectual disability and severe challenging behaviour in Victoria, Australia.' *Journal of Applied Research in Intellectual Disabilities 24,* 6, 554–65.

Coles, E. and Blunden, R. (1979) *The Establishment and Maintenance of a Ward-Based Activity Period within a Mental Handicap Hospital.* Cardiff: Mental Handicap in Wales, Applied Research Unit.

Commission for Social Care Inspection (2005) *The State of Social Care in England 2004–5.* London: Commission for Social Care Inspection.

Commission for Social Care Inspection (2006) *Handled with Care? Managing Medication for Residents of Care Homes and Children's Homes: A Follow-up Study.* London: Commission for Social Care Inspection.

Cornwall County Council Adult Protection Committee (2007) *The Murder of Steven Hoskin: Serious Case Review. Multi-Agency and Single-Agency Recommendations and Action Plans.* Truro: Cornwall County Council.

Crocker, T.M. (1990) 'Assessing client participation in mental handicap services: A pilot study.' *British Journal of Mental Subnormality 36,* 2, 98–107.

Cullen, C. (1988) 'A review of staff training: The emperor's old clothes.' *Irish Journal of Psychology 9*, 2, 309–23.

Department of Health (1991) *Research for Health: A Research and Development Strategy for the NHS.* London: Her Majesty's Stationery Office.

Department of Health (1993) *Services for People with Learning Disabilities and Challenging Behaviour or Mental Health Needs: Report of a Project Group (Chairman: Prof. J.L. Mansell).* London: Her Majesty's Stationery Office.

Department of Health (2001a) *Planning with People: Towards Person-Centred Approaches: Guidance for Implementation Groups.* London: Department of Health.

Department of Health (2001b) *Valuing People: A New Strategy for Learning Disability for the 21st Century* (Cm 5086). London: The Stationery Office.

Department of Health (2007a) *Services for People with Learning Disabilities and Challenging Behaviour or Mental Health Needs: Report of a Project Group (Chairman: Prof. J.L. Mansell)* (Revised Edition). London: Department of Health.

Department of Health (2007b) *Valuing People Now: From Progress to Transformation.* London: Department of Health.

Department of Health (2010) *Raising Our Sights: Services for Adults with Profound Intellectual and Multiple Disabilities. A Report by Professor Jim Mansell.* London: Department of Health.

Department of Health and Social Security (1979) *Report of the Committee of Enquiry into Mental Handicap Nursing and Care (Chairman: Peggy Jay)* (Cmnd 7468). London: Her Majesty's Stationery Office.

DeWaele, I., Van Loon, J., Van Hove, G. and Schalock, R.L. (2005) 'Quality of life vs. quality of care: Implications for people and programs.' *Journal of Policy and Practice in Intellectual Disabilities 2*, 229–39.

Donabedian, A. (1980) *Explorations in Quality Assessment and Monitoring (Volume 1): The Definition of Quality and Approaches to its Assessment.* Michigan: Health Administration Press.

Durward, L. and Whatmore, R. (1976) 'Testing measures of the quality of residential care: A pilot study.' *Behaviour Research and Therapy 14*, 149–57.

Dyer, S. and Quine, L. (1998) 'Predictors of job satisfaction and burnout among the direct care staff of a community learning disability service.' *Journal of Applied Research in Intellectual Disabilities 11*, 4, 320–32.

Einfeld, S.L., Tonge, B.J. and Mohr, C. (2003) *Developmental Behaviour Checklist for Adults (DBC-A).* Melbourne, Australia: Monash University.

Elliott, J. and Rose, J. (1997) 'An investigation of stress experienced by managers by community homes for people with intellectual disabilities.' *Journal of Applied Research in Intellectual Disabilities 10*, 1, 48–53.

Emerson, E. (1990) 'Consciousness-raising, science and normalisation.' *Clinical Psychology Forum,* 36–9.

Emerson, E., Barrett, S., Bell, C., Cummings, R. *et al.* (1987) *Developing Services for People with Severe Learning Difficulties and Challenging Behaviours.* Canterbury: Institute of Social and Applied Psychology.

Emerson, E., Beasley, F., Offord, G. and Mansell, J. (1992) 'Specialised housing for people with seriously challenging behaviours.' *Journal of Mental Deficiency Research 36*, 291–307.

Emerson, E., Hastings, R. and McGill, P. (1994) 'Values, Attitudes and Service Ideology.' In E. Emerson, P. McGill and J. Mansell (eds) *Severe Learning Disabilities and Challenging Behaviours: Designing High Quality Services.* London: Chapman and Hall.

Emerson, E. and Hatton, C. (1994) *Moving Out: Relocation from Hospital to Community.* London: Her Majesty's Stationery Office.

Emerson, E., Hatton, C., Robertson, J., Henderson, D. and Cooper, J. (1999a) 'A descriptive analysis of the relationships between social context, engagement and stereotypy in residential services for people with severe and complex disabilities.' *Journal of Applied Research in Intellectual Disabilities 12*, 1, 11–29.

Emerson, E., McGill, P. and Mansell, J. (eds) (1994) *Severe Learning Disabilities and Challenging Behaviours*. London: Chapman and Hall.

Emerson, E., Robertson, J., Gregory, N., Hatton, C. *et al.* (2000a) 'Quality and costs of community-based residential supports, village communities, and residential campuses in the United Kingdom.' *American Journal on Mental Retardation 105*, 2, 81–102.

Emerson, E., Robertson, J., Gregory, N., Kessissoglou, S. *et al.* (1999) *Quality and Costs of Residential Supports for People with Learning Disabilities: An Observational Study of Supports Provided to People with Severe and Complex Learning Disabilities in Residential Campuses and Dispersed Housing Schemes.* Manchester: Hester Adrian Research Centre.

Emerson, E., Robertson, J., Gregory, N., Kessissoglou, S. *et al.* (2000b) 'The quality and costs of community-based residential supports and residential campuses for people with severe and complex disabilities.' *Journal of Intellectual & Developmental Disability 25*, 4, 263–79.

Felce, D. (1994) 'Facilitated communication: Results from a number of recently published evaluations.' *British Journal of Learning Disabilities 22*, 122–6.

Felce, D., Bowley, C., Baxter, H., Jones, E., Lowe, K. and Emerson, E. (2000) 'The effectiveness of staff support: Evaluating Active Support training using a conditional probability approach.' *Research in Developmental Disabilities 21*, 243–55.

Felce, D., de Kock, U., Mansell, J. and Jenkins, J. (1984) 'Assessing mentally handicapped adults.' *British Journal of Mental Subnormality 30*, 2, 65–74.

Felce, D., de Kock, U. and Repp, A.C. (1986) 'An eco-behavioural comparison of small community-based houses and traditional large hospitals for severely and profoundly mentally handicapped adults.' *Applied Research in Mental Retardation 7*, 393–408.

Felce, D., de Kock, U., Thomas, M. and Saxby, H. (1986) 'Change in adaptive behaviour of severely and profoundly mentally handicapped adults in different residential settings.' *British Journal of Psychology 77*, 1986, 489–501.

Felce, D., Jones, E., Lowe, K. and Perry, J. (2003) 'Rational resourcing and productivity: Relationships among staff input, resident characteristics, and group home quality.' *American Journal on Mental Retardation 108*, 3, 161–72.

Felce, D., Kushlick, A. and Mansell, J. (1980) 'Evaluation of alternative residential facilities for the severely mentally handicapped in Wessex: Client engagement.' *Advances in Behaviour Research and Therapy 3*, 1, 13–18.

Felce, D., Lowe, K. and Beswick, J. (1993) 'Staff turnover in ordinary housing services for people with severe or profound mental handicaps.' *Community Care 37*, 143–52.

Felce, D., Lowe, K. and Blackman, D. (1995) 'Resident behaviour and staff interaction with people with intellectual disabilities and seriously challenging behaviour in residential services.' *Mental Handicap Research 8*, 272–95.

Felce, D., Lowe, K. and Jones, E. (2002a) 'Association between the provision characteristics and operation of supported housing services and resident outcomes.' *Journal of Applied Research in Intellectual Disabilities 15*, 4, 404–18.

Felce, D., Lowe, K. and Jones, E. (2002b) 'Staff activity in supported housing services.' *Journal of Applied Research in Intellectual Disabilities 15*, 4, 388–403.

Felce, D., Mansell, J. and Kushlick, A. (1980) 'Evaluation of alternative residential facilities for the severely mentally handicapped in Wessex: Staff performance.' *Advances in Behaviour Research and Therapy 3*, 25–30.

Felce, D. and Perry, J. (1995) 'The extent of support for ordinary living provided in staffed housing: The relationship between staffing levels, resident characteristics, staff:resident interactions and resident activity patterns.' *Social Science and Medicine 40*, 6, 799–810.

Felce, D., Perry, J., Lowe, K. and Jones, E. (2011) 'The impact of autism or severe challenging behaviour on lifestyle outcome in community housing.' *Journal of Applied Research in Intellectual Disabilities 24*, 2, 95–104.

Felce, D., Repp, A.C., Thomas, M., Ager, A. and Blunden, R. (1991) 'The relationship of staff:client ratios, interactions and residential placement.' *Research in Developmental Disabilities 12*, 315–31.

Felce, D. and Toogood, S. (1988) *Close to Home.* Kidderminster: British Institute of Mental Handicap.

Firth, G., Elford, H., Leeming, C. and Crabbe, M. (2008) 'Intensive interaction as a novel approach in social care: Care staff's views on the practice change process.' *Journal of Applied Research in Intellectual Disabilities 21, 1,* 58–69.

Fitzpatrick, J. (2010) *Personalised Support: How to Provide High-Quality Support to People with Complex and Challenging Needs: Learning from Partners for Inclusion.* London: Centre for Welfare Reform.

Flynn, R.J. and Lemay, R.A. (1999) *A Quarter-Century of Normalization and Social Role Valorization: Evolution and Impact.* Ottawa, ON: University of Ottawa Press.

Flynn, R.J. and Nitsch, K.E. (1980) *Normalization, Social Integration and Community Services.* Baltimore, MD: University Park Press.

Ford, J. and Honnor, J. (2000) 'Job satisfaction of community residential staff serving individuals with severe intellectual disabilities.' *Journal of Intellectual and Developmental Disability 25, 4,* 343–62.

Forrester-Jones, R., Jones, S., Heason, S. and Di-Terlizzi, M. (2004) 'Supported employment: A route to social networks.' *Journal of Applied Research in Intellectual Disabilities 17,* 199–208.

Foster-Johnson, L., Ferro, J. and Dunlap, G. (1994) 'Preferred curricular activities and reduced problem behaviors in students with intellectual disabilities.' *Journal of Applied Behavior Analysis 27, 3,* 493–504.

Freyhoff, G., Parker, C., Coué, M. and Greig, N. (2004) *Included in Society: Results and Recommendations of the European Research Initiative on Community-Based Residential Alternatives for Disabled People.* Brussels: Inclusion Europe.

Fryer, R.H. (2006) *Learning for a Change in Healthcare.* London: Department of Health.

Fyffe, C., McCubbery, J. and Reid, K.J. (2008) 'Initial investigation of organisational factors associated with the implementation of active support.' *Journal of Intellectual & Developmental Disability 33, 3,* 239–46.

Gifford, J. (2007) *A Study of the Work of Managers in Residential Services for People with Learning Disabilities.* Canterbury: University of Kent.

Gifford, J., Beadle-Brown, J. and Mansell, J. (2006) 'A study of the work of managers in residential services for people with intellectual disabilities. Paper presented at 2nd European Congress of the International Association for the Scientific Study of Intellectual Disabilities, 2–5 August 2006, Maastricht, Netherlands.' *Journal of Applied Research in Intellectual Disabilities 19, 3,* 229.

Goffman, E. (1968) *Asylums: Essays on the Social Situation of Mental Patients and Other Inmates.* Harmondsworth: Penguin.

Gold, M.W. (1980a) *Did I Say That? Articles and Commentary on the Try Another Way System.* Champaign, IL: Research Press.

Gold, M.W. (1980b) *Try Another Way.* Champaign, IL: Research Press.

Goldiamond, I. (1974) 'Toward a constructional approach to social problems.' *Behaviorism 2, 1,* 1–84.

Guthrie, K.S. and Beadle-Brown, J. (2006) 'Defining and measuring rapport: Implications for supporting people with complex needs.' *Tizard Learning Disability Review 11, 3,* 21–30.

Hakim, D. (2011) 'At state-run homes, abuse and impunity.' *New York Times* (13 March 2011), p.A1.

Hamelin, J.P. and Sturmey, P. (2011) 'Active support: A systematic review and evidence-based practice evaluation.' *Intellectual and Developmental Disabilities 49, 3,* 166–71.

Handy, C.B. (1985) *Understanding Organizations.* Harmondsworth: Penguin Books.

Harman, A.D. and Sanderson, H. (2008) 'How person-centred is active support?' *Journal of Intellectual and Developmental Disability 33, 3,* 271–3.

Harris, J.M., Veit, S.W., Allen, G.J. and Chinsky, J.M. (1974) 'Aide-resident ratio and ward population density as mediators of social interaction.' *American Journal of Mental Deficiency 79,* 320–6.

Hart, B. and Risley, T.R. (1976) 'Environmental Programming: Implications for the Severely Handicapped.' In H.J. Prehms and S.J. Deitz (eds) *Early Intervention for the Severely Handicapped: Programming and Accountability.* Eugene, OR: University of Oregon.

Hastings, R., Remington, B. and Hatton, C. (1995) 'Future directions for research on staff performance in services for people with learning disabilities.' *Mental Handicap Research 8*, 333–9.

Hastings, R.P., Reed, T.S. and Watts, M.J. (1997) 'Community staff causal attributions about challenging behaviours in people with intellectual disabilities.' *Journal of Applied Research in Intellectual Disabilities 10*, 3, 238–49.

Hatton, C., Brown, R., Caine, A. and Emerson, E. (1995a) 'Stressors, coping strategies and stress-related outcomes among direct care staff in staffed houses for people with learning disabilities.' *Mental Handicap Research 8*, 4, 252–71.

Hatton, C. and Emerson, E. (1998) 'Brief report: Organisational predictors of actual staff turnover in a service for people with multiple disabilities.' *Journal of Applied Research in Intellectual Disabilities 11*, 2, 166–71.

Hatton, C., Emerson, E., Rivers, M., Mason, H. *et al.* (1999) 'Factors associated with staff stress and work satisfaction in services for people with intellectual disability.' *Journal of Intellectual Disability Research 43*, 4, 253–67.

Hatton, C., Emerson, E., Robertson, J. and Henderson, D. (1995b) 'The quality and costs of residential services for adults with multiple disabilities: A comparative evaluation.' *Research in Developmental Disabilities 16*, 6, 439–60.

Hatton, C., Emerson, E., Robertson, J., Henderson, D. and Cooper, J. (1995c) 'An evaluation of the quality and costs of services for adults with severe learning disabilities and sensory impairments.' *Focus*, June, 14–16.

Henry, D., Keys, C., Balcazar, F. and Jopp, D. (1996) 'Attitudes of community-living staff members toward persons with mental retardation, mental illness, and dual diagnosis.' *Mental Retardation 34*, 6, 367–79.

Hewett, D. and Nind, M. (1998) *Interaction in Action: Reflections on the Use of Intensive Interaction.* London: David Fulton.

Hewitt, A.S., Larson, S.A., Lakin, K.C., Sauer, J. *et al.* (2004) 'Role and essential competencies of the frontline supervisors of direct support professionals in community services.' *Mental Retardation 42*, 2, 122–35.

Hewson, S. (1991) 'The evaluation of quality in a mental handicap service.' *International Journal of Health Care Quality Assurance 4*, 3, 18–22.

Hewson, S. and Walker, J. (1992) 'The use of evaluation in the development of a staffed residential service for adults with mental handicap.' *Mental Handicap Research 5*, 2,188–203.

Higgins, I. (2010) *How Should the Delivery of Active Support be Monitored?* Canterbury: Unpublished manuscript.

Horner, R.H., Dunlap, G. and Koegel, R.L. (1988) *Generalization and Maintenance: Life-Style Changes in Applied Settings.* Baltimore, MD: Paul H. Brookes.

House of Commons Social Services Committee (1985) *Community Care: With Special Reference to Adult Mentally Ill and Mentally Handicapped People.* London: Her Majesty's Stationery Office.

Houts, P.S. and Scott, R.A. (1975) *Goal Planning with Developmentally Disabled Persons: Procedures for Developing an Individualized Client Plan.* Hershey, PA: Milton S. Hershey Medical Centre.

Hughes, H. and Mansell, J. (1990) *Consultation to Camberwell Health Authority Learning Difficulties Care Group: Evaluation Report.* Canterbury: Centre for the Applied Psychology of Social Care, University of Kent.

Hughes, H. and Mansell, J. (1992) *Consultation to Camberwell Health Authority Learning Difficulties Care Group: Intervention Report.* Canterbury: Centre for the Applied Psychology of Social Care, University of Kent.

Hume, K., Loftin, R. and Lantz, J. (2009) 'Increasing independence in autism spectrum disorders: A review of three focused interventions.' *Journal of Autism and Developmental Disorders 39*, 9, 1329–38.

Jacobson, J.W. (1990) 'Regulations: Can they control staff compliance in human services systems?' *Mental Retardation 28*, 2, 77–82.

Jago, J.L., Jago, A.G. and Hart, M. (1984) 'An evaluation of the total communication approach for teaching language skills to developmentally delayed preschool children.' *Education and Training in Mental Retardation and Developmental Disabilities 19*, 3, 175–82.

Jenkins, J., Felce, D., Toogood, A., Mansell, J. and de Kock, U. (1988) *Individual Programme Planning.* Kidderminster: British Institute of Mental Handicap.

Jones, E., Felce, D., Lowe, K., Bowley, C. *et al.* (2001a) 'Evaluation of the dissemination of active support training in staffed community residences.' *American Journal on Mental Retardation 106*, 4, 344–58.

Jones, E., Felce, D., Lowe, K., Bowley, C. *et al.* (2001b) 'Evaluation of the dissemination of active support training and training trainers.' *Journal of Applied Research in Intellectual Disabilities 14*, 2, 79–99.

Jones, E., Perry, J., Lowe, K., Allen, D., Toogood, S. and Felce, D. (1996a) *Active Support: A Handbook for Planning Daily Activities and Support Arrangements for People with Learning Disabilities. Booklet 1: Overview.* Cardiff: Welsh Centre for Learning Disabilities Applied Research Unit.

Jones, E., Perry, J., Lowe, K., Allen, D., Toogood, S. and Felce, D. (1996b) *Active Support: A Handbook for Planning Daily Activities and Support Arrangements for People with Learning Disabilities. Booklet 2: Activity and Support Plans.* Cardiff: Welsh Centre for Learning Disabilities Applied Research Unit.

Jones, E., Perry, J., Lowe, K., Felce, D. *et al.* (1999) 'Opportunity and the promotion of activity among adults with severe intellectual disability living in community residences: The impact of training staff in active support.' *Journal of Intellectual Disability Research 43*, 3, 164–78.

Jones, J. (2000) 'A total communication approach towards meeting the communication needs of people with learning disabilities.' *Tizard Learning Disability Review 5*, 1, 20–6.

Jones, K., Brown, J., Cunningham, W.J., Roberts, J. and Williams, P. (1975) *Opening the Door: A Study of New Policies for the Mentally Handicapped.* London: Routledge and Kegan Paul.

Jordan, R. and Jones, G. (1999) 'Review of research into educational interventions for children with autism in UK.' *Autism 3*, 101–10.

Kazdin, A.E. (1989) *Behavior Modification in Applied Settings* (Fourth Edition). Pacific Grove, CA: Brooks/Cole Publishing Company.

Kellett, M. (2005) 'Catherine's legacy: Social communication development for individuals with profound learning difficulties and fragile life expectancies.' *British Journal of Special Education 32*, 3, 116–21.

Kern, J.K., Trivedi, M.H., Garver, C.R., Grannemann, B.D. *et al.* (2006) 'The pattern of sensory processing abnormalities in autism.' *Autism 10*, 480–94.

Kern, L., Vorndran, C.M., Hilt, A., Ringdahl, J.E., Adehnan, B.E. and Dunlap, G. (1998) 'Choice as an intervention to improve behavior: A review of the literature.' *Journal of Behavioral Education 8*, 2, 151–69.

Kincaid, D., Knoster, T., Harrower, J.K., Shannon, P. and Bustamante, S. (2002) 'Measuring the impact of positive behavior support.' *Journal of Positive Behavior Interventions 4*, 2, 109–17.

King, R.D., Raynes, N.V. and Tizard, J. (1971) *Patterns of Residential Care: Sociological Studies in Institutions for Handicapped Children.* London: Routledge and Kegan Paul.

King's Fund Centre (1980) *An Ordinary Life: Comprehensive Locally-Based Residential Services for Mentally Handicapped People.* London: King's Fund Centre.

Koegel, L.K., Koegel, R.L. and Dunlap, G. (1996) *Positive Behavioral Support: Including People with Difficult Behavior in the Community.* Baltimore, MD: Brookes.

Kordoutis, P., Kolaitis, G., Perakis, A., Papanikolopoulou, P. and Tsiantis, J. (1995) 'Change in care staff's attitudes towards people with learning disabilities following intervention at the Leros PIKPA Asylum.' *British Journal of Psychiatry 167*, Suppl. 28, 56–69.

Koritsas, S., Iacono, T., Hamilton, D. and Leighton, D. (2008) 'The effect of active support training on engagement, opportunities for choice, challenging behaviour and support needs.' *Journal of Intellectual & Developmental Disability 33*, 3, 247–56.

Kushlick, A. (1966) 'A community service for the mentally subnormal.' *Social Psychiatry 1*, 2, 73–82.

Kushlick, A. (1969) 'Care of the mentally subnormal.' *The Lancet*, 29 November, 1196–7.

Kushlick, A. (1976) 'Wessex, England.' In R.B. Kugel and A. Shearer (eds) *Changing Patterns in Residential Services for the Mentally Retarded* (Second Edition). Washington, DC: President's Committee on Mental Retardation.

Kushlick, A., Felce, D., Palmer, J. and Smith, J. (1976) *Evidence to the Committee of Inquiry into Mental Handicap Nursing and Care from the Health Care Evaluation Research Team Winchester.* Southampton: Health Care Evaluation Research Team (HCERT).

Lakin, K.C., Bruininks, R.H., Hill, B.K. and Hauber, F.A. (1982) 'Turnover of direct-care staff in a national sample of residential facilities for mentally retarded people.' *American Journal of Mental Deficiency 87*, 1, 64–72.

Lambert, J.L. (1975) 'Extinction by retarded children following discrimination learning with and without errors.' *American Journal of Mental Deficiency 80*, 3, 286–91.

Landesman-Dwyer, S., Sackett, G.P. and Kleinman, J.S. (1980) 'Relationship of size to resident and staff behavior in small community residences.' *American Journal of Mental Deficiency 85*, 1, 6–17.

Larson, S.A., Doljanac, R., Nord, D.K., Salmi, P., Hewitt, A.S. and O'Nell, S. (2007) *National Validation Study of Competencies for Frontline Supervisors and Direct Support Professionals: Final Report.* Minneapolis, MN: University of Minnesota, Research and Training Center on Community Integration.

Larson, S.A. and Hewitt, A.S. (2005) *Staff Recruitment, Retention, and Training Strategies for Community Human Services Organizations.* Baltimore, MD: Paul H. Brookes.

LaVigna, G.W. (1994) *The Periodic Service Review: A Total Quality Assurance System for Human Services and Education.* Baltimore, MD: Paul H. Brookes.

LaVigna, G.W. and Donellan, A.M. (1986) *Alternatives to Punishment: Solving Behavior Problems with Non-Aversive Strategies.* New York, NY: Irvington.

LaVigna, G.W., Willis, T.J. and Donellan, A.M. (1989) 'The Role of Positive Programming in Behavioral Treatment.' In E. Cipani (ed.) *The Treatment of Severe Behavior Disorders.* Washington, DC: American Association on Mental Retardation.

Leadbeater, C. (2004) *Personalisation through Participation: A New Script for Public Services.* London: Demos.

Leaning, B. and Watson, T. (2006) 'From the inside looking out: An Intensive Interaction group for people with profound and multiple learning disabilities.' *British Journal of Learning Disabilities 34*, 2, 103–9.

LeLaurin, K. and Risley, T.R. (1972) 'The organisation of day-care environments: "Zone" vs "man-to-man" staff assignments.' *Journal of Applied Behavior Analysis 5*, 225–32.

Levy, P.H., Levy, J.M. and Samowitz, P. (1994) 'Training Staff on Quality of Life Issues.' In D. Goode (ed.) *Quality of Life for Persons with Disabilities: International Perspectives and Issues.* Cambridge, MA: Brookline Books, pp.250–9.

Luiselli, J.K. and Cameron, M.J. (1998) *Antecedent Control: Innovative Approaches to Behavioural Support.* Baltimore, MD: Paul H. Brookes.

McBrien, J. and Weightman, J. (1980) 'The effect of room management procedures on engagement of profoundly handicapped children.' *British Journal of Mental Subnormality 26*, 38–53.

McClannahan, L.E. and Risley, T.R. (1975) 'Design of living environments for nursing-home residents: Increasing participation in recreation activities.' *Journal of Applied Behavior Analysis 8*, 3, 261–8.

McConkey, R., Morris, I. and Purcell, M. (1999) 'Communications between staff and adults with intellectual disabilities in naturally occurring settings.' *Journal of Intellectual Disability Research 43*, 3, 194–205.

McCubbery, J. and Fyffe, C. (2006) *Evaluation of Active Support Pilot Project.* Melbourne, Australia: Victorian Department of Human Services.

McGee, J.J., Menolascino, F.J., Hobbs, D.C. and Menousek, P.E. (1987) *Gentle Teaching: A Non-Aversive Approach to Helping Persons with Mental Retardation.* New York, NY: Human Sciences Press.

McLaughlin, D.M. and Carr, E.G. (2005) 'Quality of rapport as a setting event for problem behavior.' *Journal of Positive Behavior Interventions 7,* 2, 68–91.

McVilly, K.R., Gelman, S., Leighton, D. and O'Nell, S. (2011) *Active Support: Organisational Preparation and Implementation.* Melbourne, Australia: Jewish Care.

Mansell, J. (1988a) *Staffed Housing for People with Mental Handicaps: Achieving Widespread Dissemination.* Bexhill/Bristol: South East Thames Regional Health Authority/National Health Service Training Authority.

Mansell, J. (1988b) 'Training for Service Development.' In D. Towell (ed.) *An Ordinary Life in Practice: Lessons from the Experience of Developing Comprehensive Community-Based Services for People with Learning Disabilities.* London: King's Fund Centre.

Mansell, J. (1989) 'Evaluation of training in the development of staffed housing for people with mental handicaps.' *Mental Handicap Research 2,* 137–51.

Mansell, J. (1994) 'Specialized group homes for persons with severe or profound mental retardation and serious problem behaviour in England.' *Research in Developmental Disabilities 15,* 371–88.

Mansell, J. (1995) 'Staffing and staff performance in services for people with severe or profound learning disability and serious challenging behaviour.' *Journal of Intellectual Disability Research 39,* 3–14.

Mansell, J. (2006) 'Deinstitutionalisation and community living: Progress, problems and priorities.' *Journal of Intellectual and Developmental Disability 31,* 2, 65–76.

Mansell, J. and Barrett, S. (1993) *An Audit of Southwark Social Services for People with Learning Disabilities: Final Report.* Canterbury: Centre for the Applied Psychology of Social Care (now the Tizard Centre).

Mansell, J. and Beadle-Brown, J. (2004a) 'Person-centred planning or person-centred action? A response to the commentaries.' *Journal of Applied Research in Intellectual Disabilities 17,* 31–5.

Mansell, J. and Beadle-Brown, J. (2004b) 'Person-centred planning or person-centred action? Policy and practice in intellectual disability services.' *Journal of Applied Research in Intellectual Disabilities 17,* 1–9.

Mansell, J. and Beadle-Brown, J. (2010) 'Deinstitutionalisation and community living: Position statement of the Comparative Policy and Practice Special Interest Research Group of the International Association for the Scientific Study of Intellectual Disabilities.' *Journal of Intellectual Disability Research 54,* 2, 104–12.

Mansell, J. and Beadle-Brown, J. (2011) 'Estimating activity duration by momentary time-sampling of part or all of the day.' *Journal of Applied Research in Intellectual Disabilities 24,* 489–94.

Mansell, J., Beadle-Brown, J., Ashman, B. and Ockendon, J. (2005) *Person-Centred Active Support: A Multi-Media Training Resource for Staff to Enable Participation, Inclusion and Choice for People with Learning Disabilities.* Brighton: Pavilion.

Mansell, J., Beadle-Brown, J., Bigby, C., Mountford, L. and Clement, T. (2011) *Active Support Implementation in Victoria: Report to Chief Executives.* Melbourne, Australia: La Trobe University.

Mansell, J., Beadle-Brown, J., Macdonald, S. and Ashman, B. (2003) 'Resident involvement in activity in small community homes for people with learning disabilities.' *Journal of Applied Research in Intellectual Disabilities 16,* 1, 63–74.

Mansell, J., Beadle-Brown, J., Whelton, R., Beckett, C. and Hutchinson, A. (2008) 'Effect of service structure and organisation on staff care practices in small community homes for people with intellectual disabilities.' *Journal of Applied Research in Intellectual Disabilities 21,* 3, 398–413.

Mansell, J. and Beasley, F. (1993) 'Small staffed houses for people with a severe mental handicap and challenging behaviour.' *British Journal of Social Work 23,* 329–44.

Mansell, J., Brown, H., McGill, P., Hoskin, S., Lindley, P. and Emerson, E. (1987a) *Bringing People Back Home: A Staff Training Initiative in Mental Handicap.* Bristol and Bexhill: National Health Service Training Authority and South East Thames Regional Health Authority.

Mansell, J. and Elliott, T. (2001) 'Staff members' prediction of consequences for their work in residential settings.' *American Journal on Mental Retardation 106*, 5, 424–47.

Mansell, J., Elliott, T., Beadle-Brown, J., Ashman, B. and Macdonald, S. (2002) 'Engagement in meaningful activity and "active support" of people with intellectual disabilities in residential care.' *Research in Developmental Disabilities 23*, 5, 342–52.

Mansell, J. and Elliott, T.E. (1996) *Active Support Measure.* Canterbury: Tizard Centre.

Mansell, J., Felce, D., de Kock, U. and Jenkins, J. (1982a) 'Increasing purposeful activity of severely and profoundly mentally-handicapped adults.' *Behaviour Research and Therapy 20*, 593–604.

Mansell, J., Felce, D., Jenkins, J. and de Kock, U. (1982b) 'Increasing staff ratios in an activity with severely mentally handicapped people.' *British Journal of Mental Subnormality 28*, 2, 97–9.

Mansell, J., Felce, D., Jenkins, J., de Kock, U. and Toogood, A. (1987b) *Developing Staffed Housing for People with Mental Handicaps.* Tunbridge Wells: Costello.

Mansell, J., Felce, D., Jenkins, J., de Kock, U. and Toogood, A. (1987c) 'Enabling Individual Participation.' In *Developing Staffed Housing for People with Mental Handicaps.* Tunbridge Wells: Costello, pp.197–231.

Mansell, J., Hughes, H. and McGill, P. (1994) 'Maintaining Local Residential Placements.' In E. Emerson, P. McGill and J. Mansell (eds) *Severe Learning Disabilities and Challenging Behaviour: Designing High-Quality Services.* London: Chapman and Hall, pp.260–81.

Mansell, J., Jenkins, J., Felce, D. and de Kock, U. (1984) 'Measuring the activity of severely and profoundly mentally handicapped adults in ordinary housing.' *Behaviour Research and Therapy 22*, 1, 23–9.

Mansell, J., McGill, P. and Emerson, E. (2001) 'Development and Evaluation of Innovative Residential Services for People with Severe Intellectual Disability and Serious Challenging Behaviour.' In L.M. Glidden (ed.) *International Review of Research in Mental Retardation* (Vol. 24). New York, NY: Academic Press.

Martin, J.P. (1984) *Hospitals in Trouble.* Oxford: Basil Blackwell.

Marvin, C. (1998) 'Teaching and Learning for Children with Profound and Multiple Learning Difficulties.' In P. Lacey and C. Ouvry (eds) *People with Profound and Multiple Learning Disabilities: A Collaborative Approach to Meeting Complex Needs.* London: David Fulton.

Meichenbaum, D. (1977) *Cognitive-Behavior Modification: An Integrative Approach.* New York, NY: Plenum.

Mental Disability Advocacy Center and Association for Social Affirmation of People with Mental Disabilities (2003) *Cage Beds: Inhuman and Degrading Treatment in Four EU Accession Countries.* Budapest, Hungary: Mental Disability Advocacy Center.

Mental Disability Advocacy Center and Association for Social Affirmation of People with Mental Disabilities (2011) *Out of Sight: Human Rights in Psychiatric Hospitals and Social Care Institutions in Croatia.* Budapest, Hungary: Mental Disability Advocacy Center.

Mesibov, G.B. (1997) 'Formal and informal measures of the effectiveness of the TEACCH programme.' *Autism 1*, 25–35.

Mesibov, G.B., Shea, V. and Schopler, E. (2004) *The TEACCH Approach to Autism Spectrum Disorders.* London: Springer.

Moore, J. and Mansell, J. (1998) *Residential Services for People with Learning Disabilities Provided by the London Borough of Southwark: Five-Year Follow-Up.* Canterbury: Tizard Centre.

Morgan, B.B., Salas, E. and Glickman, A.S. (1994) 'An analysis of team evolution and maturation.' *The Journal of General Psychology 120*, 3, 277–91.

Morris, P. (1969) *Put Away.* London: Routledge and Kegan Paul.

Mount, B. and Zwernik, K. (1988) *It's Never Too Early, It's Never Too Late: A Booklet about Personal Futures Planning.* St Paul, MN: Governor's Planning Council on Developmental Disabilities.

Mudford, O.C. (1995) 'Review of the gentle teaching data.' *American Journal on Mental Retardation 99*, 4, 345–55.

Murphy, G.H. and Clare, I.C.H. (1995) 'Adults' Capacity to Make Decisions Affecting the Person: Psychologists' Contribution.' In R.H.C. Bull and D.C. Carson (eds) *Psychology in Legal Contexts.* Chichester: Wiley.

Netten, A., Beadle-Brown, J., Trukeschitz, B., Towers, A. *et al.* (2010) *Measuring the Outcomes of Care Homes: Final Report* (Discussion Paper 2696/2). Canterbury: Personal Social Services Research Unit, University of Kent.

Nihira, K., Leland, H. and Lambert, N. (1993) *AAMR Adaptive Behavior Scale: Residential and Community* (Second Edition). Austin, TX: Pro-Ed.

Nind, M. (1996) 'Efficacy of intensive interaction: Developing sociability and communication in people with severe and complex learning difficulties using an approach based on caregiver–infant interaction.' *European Journal of Special Educational Needs 11*, 1, 48–66.

Nind, M. and Hewett, D. (1994) *Access to Communication: Developing the Basics of Communication with People with Severe Learning Difficulties through Intensive Interaction.* London: David Fulton.

Nind, M. and Hewett, D. (2001) *A Practical Guide to Intensive Interaction.* Kidderminster: BILD Publications.

Noone, S.J. and Hastings, R. (2010) 'Using acceptance and mindfulness-based workshops with support staff caring for adults with intellectual disabilities.' *Mindfulness 1*, 2, 67–73.

O'Brien, J. (1987) 'A Guide to Life-Style Planning.' In G.T. Bellamy and B. Wilcox (eds) *A Comprehensive Guide to the Activities Catalog: An Alternative Curriculum for Youths and Adults with Severe Disabilities.* Baltimore, MD: Paul H. Brookes.

O'Brien, J. (undated) *An Ethics of Possibility.* Toronto, ON: Inclusion Press.

O'Brien, J. and Lovett, H. (1992) *Finding A Way Toward Everyday Lives: The Contribution of Person Centered Planning.* Harrisburg, PA: Pennsylvania Office of Mental Retardation.

O'Brien, C.L. and O'Brien, J. (2000) 'The Origins of Person-Centered Planning: A Community of Practice Perspective.' In S. Holburn and P. Vietze (eds) *Person-Centered Planning: Research, Practice, and Future Directions.* Baltimore, MD: Paul H. Brookes.

O'Brien, J., O'Brien, C.L. and Schwartz, D.B. (1990) *What Can We Count on to Make and Keep People Safe? Perspectives on Creating Effective Safeguards for People with Developmental Disabilities.* Lithonia, GA: Responsive Systems Associates.

O'Neill, R., Horner, R., Albin, R., Storey, K. and Sprague, J. (1990) *Functional Analysis: A Practical Assessment Guide.* Sycamore, IL: Sycamore Publishing Company.

Orlowska, D. and Mansell, J. (1996) *Second Audit of Southwark Residential Services for People with Learning Disabilities.* Canterbury: Tizard Centre.

Orthner, D.K. and Bownen, G.L. (2004) 'Strengthening Practice through Results Management.' In A.R. Roberts and K. Yaeger (eds) *Handbook of Practice-Based Research.* New York, NY: Oxford University Press.

Orthner, D.K., Cook, P., Sabah, Y. and Rosenfeld, J. (2006) 'Organization learning: A cross-national pilot test of effectiveness in children's services.' *Evaluation and Program Planning 29*, 7–78.

Ozonoff, S. and Cathcart, K. (1998) 'Effectiveness of home program intervention for young children with autism.' *Journal of Autism and Developmental Disorders 28*, 25–32.

Panerai, S., Fernante, L., Caputo, V. and Impellizeri, C. (1998) 'Use of structured teaching for treatment of children with autism and severe profound mental retardation.' *Education and Training in Mental Retardation and Developmental Disabilities 33*, 367–74.

Panerai, S., Ferrante, L. and Zingale, M. (2002) 'Benefits of the treatment and education of autistic and communication handicapped children (TEACCH) programme as compared with a non-specific approach.' *Journal of Intellectual Disability Research 46*, 318–27.

Pearpoint, J., O'Brien, J. and Forest, M. (1993) *PATH: A Workbook for Planning Positive, Possible Futures and Planning Alternative Tomorrows with Hope for Schools, Organizations, Businesses and Families.* Toronto, ON: Inclusion Press.

Perry, J. and Felce, D. (2003) 'Quality of life outcomes for people with intellectual disabilities living in staffed community housing services: A stratified random sample of statutory, voluntary and private agency provision.' *Journal of Applied Research in Intellectual Disabilities 16*, 1, 11–28.

Perry, J., Felce, D., Allen, D. and Meek, A. (2011) 'Resettlement outcomes for people with severe challenging behaviour moving from institutional to community living.' *Journal of Applied Research in Intellectual Disabilities 24*, 1–17.

Person, B. (2000) 'Brief report: A longitudinal study of quality of life and independence among adult men with autism.' *Journal of Autism and Developmental Disorders 30*, 61–6.

Peters, T.J. and Waterman, R.H. (1982) *In Search of Excellence: Lessons from America's Best-Run Companies.* New York, NY: Harper and Row Publishers.

Porterfield, J. and Blunden, R. (1979) *Establishing Activity Periods in Special Needs Rooms Within Adult Training Centres: A Replication Study.* Cardiff: Mental Handicap in Wales, Applied Research Unit.

Porterfield, J., Blunden, R. and Blewitt, E. (1980) 'Improving environments for profoundly handicapped adults: Using prompts and social attention to maintain high group engagement.' *Behavior Modification 4*, 225–41.

Potts, M., Halliday, S., Plimley, C., Wright, J. and Cuthbertson, A. (1995) 'Staff stress and satisfaction in small staffed houses in the community: 1.' *British Journal of Nursing 4*, 8, 452–9.

Productivity Commission (2011) *Disability Care and Support: Inquiry Report No. 54.* Canberra, Australia: Productivity Commission.

Purcell, M., Morris, I. and McConkey, R. (1999) 'Staff perceptions of the communicative competence of adult persons with intellectual disabilities.' *British Journal of Developmental Disabilities 45*, 88, 16–25.

Queensland Government (2007) *Investing in Positive Futures: The Queensland Government's Response to a Report by the Honourable W.J. Carter QC, Challenging Behaviours and Disability – A Targeted Response.* Brisbane, Australia: Disability Services Queensland.

Quilitch, H.R. (1974) 'Purposeful activity increased on a geriatric ward through programmed recreation.' *Journal of the American Geriatrics Society XXII*, 5, 226–9.

Quilitch, H.R. and Gray, J.D. (1974) 'Purposeful activity for the PMR: A demonstration project.' *Mental Retardation*, December, 28–9.

Quinn, J.B. (1980) *Strategies for Change: Logical Incrementalism.* Homewood, IL: Richard D. Irwin.

Reid, D.H. and Whitman, T.L. (1983) 'Behavioral staff management in institutions: A critical review of effectiveness and acceptability.' *Analysis and Intervention in Developmental Disabilities 3*, 2–3, 131–49.

Rice, D.M. and Rosen, M. (1991) 'Direct-care staff: A neglected priority.' *Mental Retardation 29*, 4, iii–iv.

Richardson, G. (1990) *Feedback in Social Science and Systems Theory.* Philadelphia, PN: University of Pennsylvania Press.

Riches, V.C., Harman, A.D., Keen, D., Pennell, D., Harley, J.H. and Walker, M. (2011) 'Transforming staff practice through active support.' *Journal of Intellectual and Developmental Disability 36*, 3, 156–66.

Rioux, M.H. (1997) 'Disability: The place of judgement in a world of fact.' *Journal of Intellectual Disability Research 41*, 2, 102–11.

Risley, T.R. (1996) 'Get a Life! Positive Behavioral Intervention for Challenging Behaviour through Life Arrangement and Life Coaching.' In L.K. Koegel, R.L. Koegel and G. Dunlap (eds) *Positive Behavioral Support: Including People with Difficult Behavior in the Community.* Baltimore, MD: Brookes.

Robertson, J., Emerson, E., Gregory, N., Hatton, C. *et al.* (2001) 'Social networks of people with mental retardation in residential settings.' *Mental Retardation 39*, 3, 201–14.

Robertson, J., Emerson, E., Hatton, C., Elliott, J. *et al.* (2005) *The Impact of Person-Centred Planning.* Lancaster: Institute for Health Research, Lancaster University.

Rose, J. (1995) 'Stress and residential staff: Towards an integration of existing research.' *Mental Handicap Research 8*, 220–36.

Rose, J. (1997) 'Stress and stress management among residential care staff.' *Tizard Learning Disability Review 2*, 1, 8–15.

Samuel, J., Nind, M., Volans, A. and Scriven, I. (2008) 'An evaluation of Intensive Interaction in community living settings for adults with profound intellectual disabilities.' *Journal of Intellectual Disabilities 12*, 2, 111–26.

Sanderson, H. (2000) Person-Centred Planning: Key Features and Approaches. Available at www.familiesleadingplanning.co.uk/Documents/PCP%20Key%20Features%20and%20Styles.pdf, accessed on 2 December 2011.

Sanderson, H., Jones, E. and Brown, K. (2002) 'Active support and person-centred planning: Strange bedfellows or ideal partners?' *Tizard Learning Disability Review 7*, 1, 31–8.

Sanderson, H., Kennedy, J. and Ritchie, P. (1996) *People, Plans and Possibilities: Exploring Person-Centred Planning*. Edinburgh: SHS.

Sanderson, H. and Smull, M.W. (2011) *Person-Centred Thinking and Planning*. Stockport: Helen Sanderson Associates.

Sapieras, P. and Beadle-Brown, J. (2006) 'The effectiveness of TEACCH approach programme for people with autism in Greece.' *Autism 10*, 4, 330–43.

Saunders, R.R. and Saunders, M.D. (1998) 'Supported Routines.' In J.K. Luiselli and M.J. Cameron (eds) *Antecedent Control: Innovative Approaches to Behavioural Support*. Baltimore, MD: Paul H. Brookes.

Saxby, H., Thomas, M., Felce, D. and de Kock, U. (1986) 'The use of shops, cafes and public houses by severely and profoundly mentally handicapped adults.' *British Journal of Mental Subnormality 32*, 69–81.

Schalock, R.L., Brown, I., Brown, R., Cummins, R.A. *et al.* (2002) 'Conceptualization, measurement, and application of quality of life for persons with intellectual disabilities: Report of an international panel of experts.' *Mental Retardation 40*, 6, 457–70.

Schalock, R.L., Gardner, J.F. and Bradley, V.J. (2007) *Quality of Life of Persons with Intellectual and Other Developmental Disabilities: Applications across Individuals, Organizations, Systems, and Communities*. Washington, DC: American Association on Intellectual and Developmental Disabilities.

Schalock, R.L., Verdugo, M.A., Bonham, G.S., Fantova, F. and Van Loon, J. (2008) 'Enhancing personal outcomes: Organizational strategies, guidelines, and examples.' *Journal of Policy and Practice in Intellectual Disabilities 5*, 4, 276–85.

Schopler, E., Mesibov, G.B., DeVellis, R.F. and Short, A. (1981) 'Treatment Outcome for Autistic Children and Their Families.' In P. Mittler (ed.) *Frontiers of Knowledge in Mental Retardation: Social, Educational and Behavioral Aspects*. Baltimore, MD: University Park Press.

Senge, P.M. (2006) *The Fifth Discipline: The Art and Practice of the Learning Organization*. London: Random House Business.

Sheldon, B. and Chilvers, R. (2000) *Evidence-Based Social Care: A Study of Prospects and Problems*. Lyme Regis: Russell House.

Singh, N.N., Lancioni, G.E., Winton, A.S.W., Adkins, A.D., Singh, A.N. and Singh, J. (2011) 'Mindfulness-Based Approaches.' In J.L. Taylor, W.R. Lindsay, R.P. Hastings and C. Hatton (eds) *Psychological Therapies for Adults with Intellectual Disabilities*. Chichester: Wiley-Blackwell.

Singh, N.N., Lancioni, G.E., Winton, A.S.W., Curtis, W.J. *et al.* (2006) 'Mindful staff increase learning and reduce aggression in adults with developmental disabilities.' *Research in Developmental Disabilities 27*, 5, 545–58.

Singh, N.N., Lancioni, G.E., Winton, A.S.W., Wahler, R.G., Singh, J. and Sage, M. (2004) 'Mindful caregiving increases happiness among individuals with profound multiple disabilities.' *Research in Developmental Disabilities 25*, 2, 207–18.

Smith, C., Felce, D., Jones, E. and Lowe, K. (2002) 'Responsiveness to staff support: Evaluating the impact of individual characteristics on the effectiveness of active support training using a conditional probability approach.' *Journal of Intellectual Disability Research 46*, 594–604.

Smull, M.W. and Burke-Harrison, S. (1992) *Supporting People with Severe Reputations in the Community*. Alexandria, VA: National Association of State Mental Retardation Program Directors.

Stancliffe, R.J. (1997) 'Community living unit size, staff presence, and residents' choice making.' *Mental Retardation 35*, 1, 1–9.

Stancliffe, R.J., Harman, A., Toogood, S. and McVilly, K.R. (2007) 'Australian implementation and evaluation of active support.' *Journal of Applied Research in Intellectual Disabilities 20*, 3, 211–27.

Stancliffe, R.J., Harman, A.D., Toogood, S. and McVilly, K.R. (2008a) 'Staff behaviour and resident engagement before and after active support training.' *Journal of Intellectual & Developmental Disability 33*, 3, 257–70.

Stancliffe, R.J., Jones, E. and Mansell, J. (2008) 'Research in active support.' *Journal of Intellectual & Developmental Disability 33*, 3, 194–5.

Stancliffe, R.J., Jones, E., Mansell, J. and Lowe, K. (2008b) 'Active support: A critical review and commentary.' *Journal of Intellectual & Developmental Disability 33*, 3, 196–214.

Stancliffe, R.J., McVilly, K.R., Radler, G., Mountford, L. and Tomaszewski, P. (2010) 'Active Support, Participation and Depression.' *Journal of Applied Research in Intellectual Disabilities 23*, 4, 312–21.

Stenfert Kroese, B. and Fleming, I. (1992) 'Staff's attitudes and working conditions in community-based group homes of people with mental handicaps.' *Mental Handicap Research 5*, 1, 82–91.

Stokes, T. and Baer, D. (1977) 'An implicit technology of generalization.' *Journal of Applied Behavior Analysis 10*, 349–67.

Szalai, A. (ed.) (1972) *The Use of Time: Daily Activities of Urban and Suburban Populations in Twelve Countries*. The Hague, Netherlands: Mouton.

Szivos, S. (1991) 'Consciousness-raising: An attempt to redress the more repressive aspects of normalisation, but not its more positive ones.' *Clinical Psychology Forum, 33*, 28–31.

Szivos, S.E. and Griffiths, E. (1990) 'Consciousness-raising and social identity theory: A challenge to normalisation.' *Clinical Psychology Forum, 28*, 11–15.

Szivos, S.E. and Travers, E. (1988) 'Consciousness raising among mentally handicapped people: A critique of the implications of normalization.' *Human Relations 41*, 9, 641–53.

Tajfel, H. and Turner, J.C. (1986) 'The Social Identity Theory of Intergroup Behavior.' In S. Worchel and L.W. Austin (eds) *Psychology of Intergroup Relations*. Chicago, IL: Nelson-Hall.

Taylor, S.J. (1988) 'Caught in the continuum: A critical analysis of the principle of the least restrictive environment.' *Journal of the Association for Persons with Severe Handicaps 13*, 1, 41–53.

Thousand, J.S., Burchard, S.N. and Hasazi, J.E. (1986) 'Field-based generation and social validation of managers and staff competencies for small community residences.' *Applied Research in Mental Retardation 7*, 263–83.

Tizard, J. (1960) 'Residential care of mentally handicapped children.' *British Medical Journal, 5178*, 1041–6.

Toogood, A. (2000) 'Ten years of providing intensive support services for people with learning disabilities and challenging behaviour: A brief service description and review.' *Tizard Learning Disability Review 5*, 3, 14–22.

Toogood, S. (2008) 'Interactive training.' *Journal of Intellectual & Developmental Disability 33*, 3, 215–24.

Toogood, S., Boyd, S., Bell, A. and Salisbury, H. (2011) 'Self-injury and other challenging behaviour at intervention and ten years on: A case study.' *Tizard Learning Disability Review 16*, 1, 18–29.

Tossebro, J. (1995) 'Impact of size revisited: Relation of number of residents to self-determination and deprivatization.' *American Journal on Mental Retardation 100*, 1, 59–67.

Totsika, V., Felce, D., Kerr, M. and Hastings, R.P. (2010). 'Behavior problems, psychiatric symptoms, and quality of life for older adults with intellectual disability with and without autism.' *Journal of Autism and Developmental Disorders 40*, 10, 1171–8.

Totsika, V., Toogood, S. and Hastings, R. (2008) 'Active Support: Development, Evidence Base, and Future Directions.' In L.M. Glidden (ed.) *International Review of Research in Mental Retardation* (Volume 35). London: Elsevier.

Totsika, V., Toogood, S., Hastings, R. and McCarthy, J. (2010) 'The effect of active support interactive training on the daily lives of adults with an intellectual disability.' *Journal of Applied Research in Intellectual Disabilities 23*, 112–21.

Totsika, V., Toogood, S., Hastings, R.P. and Nash, S. (2008) 'Interactive training for active support: Perspectives from staff.' *Journal of Intellectual & Developmental Disability 33*, 3, 22–38.

Touchette, P.E. (1968) 'The effects of a graduated stimulus change on the acquisition of a simple discrimination in severely retarded boys.' *Journal of the Experimental Analysis of Behavior 11*, 1, 39–48.

Tuckman, B.W. (1965) 'Developmental sequence in small groups.' *Psychological Bulletin 63*, 384–99.

United Nations (2006) *Convention on the Rights of Persons with Disabilities*. New York, NY: United Nations.

van Oorsouw, W., Embregts, P., Bosman, A. and Jahoda, A. (2009) 'Training staff serving clients with intellectual disabilities: A meta-analysis of aspects determining effectiveness.' *Research in Developmental Disabilities 30*, 503–11.

Vandercook, T., York, J. and Forest, M. (1989) 'The McGill Action Planning System (MAPS): A strategy for building the vision.' *Journal of the Association for Persons with Severe Handicaps 14*, 205–15.

Vygotsky, L.S. (1978) *Mind in Society: The Development of Higher Psychological Processes* (trans. M. Cole). Cambridge, MA: Harvard University Press.

Walsh, P.N., Emerson, E., Bradley, V., Schalock, R.L. and Moseley, C. (2007) *Supported Accommodation Services for People with Intellectual Disabilities*. Dublin: National Disability Authority.

Watson, J. and Fisher, A. (1997) 'Evaluating the effectiveness of intensive interactive teaching with pupils with profound and complex learning difficulties.' *British Journal of Special Education 24*, 2, 80–7.

Welsh Office (1983) *All Wales Strategy for the Development of Services for Mentally Handicapped People*. Cardiff: Her Majesty's Stationery Office.

Whiffen, P. (1984) *Initiatives in In-Service Training: Helping Staff to Care for Mentally Handicapped People in the Community* (Paper 5.2). London: Central Council for Education and Training in Social Work.

Wilcox, B. and Bellamy, G.T. (1987a) *The Activities Catalog: An Alternative Curriculum for Youth and Adults with Severe Disabilities*. Baltimore, MD: Paul H. Brookes.

Wilcox, B. and Bellamy, G.T. (1987b) *A Comprehensive Guide to The Activities Catalog: An Alternative Curriculum for Youth and Adults with Severe Disabilities*. Baltimore, MD: Paul H. Brookes.

Willer, B. and Intagliata, J. (1984) 'An overview of the social policy of deinstitutionalization.' *International Review of Research in Mental Retardation 12*, 1–23.

Winett, R.A. and Winkler, R.C. (1972) 'Current behavior modification in the classroom: Be still, be quiet, be docile.' *Journal of Applied Behavior Analysis 5*, 4, 499–504.

Wing, J.K. and Brown, G.W. (1970) *Institutionalism and Schizophrenia: A Comparative Study of Three Mental Hospitals 1960–1968*. London: Cambridge University Press.

Wolfensberger, W. (1975) *The Origin and Nature of Our Institutional Models*. Syracuse, NY: Human Policy Press.

Wolfensberger, W. (1980) 'The Definition of Normalization: Update, Problems, Disagreements and Misunderstandings.' In R.J. Flynn and K.E. Nitsch (eds) *Normalization, Social Integration and Community Services*. Baltimore, MD: University Park Press.

Wolfensberger, W. (1984) 'Social role valorization: A proposed new term for the principle of normalization.' *Mental Retardation 21*, 234–9.

Wolfensberger, W. (2000) 'A brief overview of social role valorization.' *Mental Retardation 38*, 2, 105–23.

Wolfensberger, W. and Glenn, L. (1975) *Program Analysis of Service Systems: A Method for the Quantitative Evaluation of Human Services*. Toronto, ON: National Institute on Mental Retardation.

Wolfensberger, W. and Thomas, S. (1983) *PASSING: Programme Analysis of Service Systems' Implementation of Normalization Goals*. Toronto, ON: National Institute on Mental Retardation.

Subject Index

Author Index